D0340667

BREAKTHRU PUBLISHING

P.O.BOX 2866

HOUSTON, TEXAS 77252-2866

713-522-7660

60 Minutes and the Assassination of Werner Erhard

How America's Top Rated Television Show Was Used In An Attempt To Destroy A Man Who Was Making A Difference

By Jane Self, Ph.D.

CONCORDIA UNIVERSITY LIBRARY
PORTLAND, OR 97211

OTHER RECOMMENDED BOOKS AND TAPES
BY BREAKTHRU PUBLISHING

DIETS DON'T WORK...The Secrets of Losing Weight Step-By-Step When All Else Fails by Dr. Bob Schwartz, Ph.D.. This New York Times Best Seller is recommended by universities and physicians all over the United States, Canada, and England. Perfect for anyone that is struggling with their weight or eating and has failed to lose their weight and keep it off by dieting.   Only $9.95

DIETS DON'T WORK AUDIO TAPES...Two cassette audio album.
                                                    Only $19.95

DIETS DON'T WORK VIDEO PROGRAM (VHS)...80 minute "Live" seminar   Only $29.95

DIETS STILL DON'T WORK...How To Lose Weight Step-By-Step Even After You've Failed At Dieting by Dr. Bob Schwartz, Ph.D.. This is the continuation of *DIETS DON'T WORK*. Contains additional discoveries about losing weight without dieting.   Only $9.95,

THE 14 DAY STRESS CURE...A New Approach For Dealing With Stress That Can Change Your Life by Dr. Mort Orman, M.D.. Stress kills. Without changing the circumstances, Dr. Orman shows the reader how to get rid of every kind of stress. The reader will quickly notice an increase in their energy, health, sex drive, well being, and productivity from reading just one chapter a day.   Only $13.95

FREE SHIPPING AND HANDLING

Just indicate with your order that you have read *ANY OF OUR BOOKS* and the shipping and handling charges will be waived. (Texas residents add 8 % for sales tax.)

For quotes on quantity discounts for any of our books, either for resale or to give away as gifts, or to order by credit card...
call 1-800-227-1152.

To order by check... Send your check to:

BREAKTHRU PUBLISHING
P.O.BOX 2866
HOUSTON, TEXAS 77252-2866

60 MINUTES AND THE ASSASSINATION OF WERNER ERHARD

COPYRIGHT © 1992 BY JANE SELF

ISBN 0-942540-23-9
1 2 3 4 5 6 7 8 9 10/98 97 96 95 94 93 92

All rights reserved. No part of this book may be reproduced in whole or in part in a retrieval system or transmitted in any form by an electronic, mechanical, photocopying, recording means or otherwise, without permission in writing from the author and publisher.

Published by
BREAKTHRU PUBLISHING
Houston, Texas
1992
Printed in the United States of America

TABLE OF CONTENTS

CHAPTER I
SETTING THE STAGE

It was well past midnight when the ringing of the telephone jerked me out of a deep sleep. On the other end, an excited voice urged me to drop everything and jump on a plane to New York the next day.

"Janie, I know this is outrageous, but you've got to come up here tomorrow night. I've had the most incredible experience and I want you to be a part of it." The voice belonged to my brother, Jim.

I was living in Roberta, Georgia, a small town 90 miles southwest of Atlanta, and working in nearby Macon as assistant features editor at *The Macon Telegraph*. Unsure of whether or not Jim was really serious, I patiently explained to him that I couldn't take off from work on such short notice and that I had no money for an airplane ticket.

"Put it on your credit card and call in an emergency. This is very important—and it will change your life. You'll never be the same," he insisted. And he was definitely serious.

The exchange went on about 10 more minutes until Jim finally accepted my refusal. But I was fascinated. I had never seen him so fired up and so assertive. The next morning, I called my older sister to see what was going on.

Jim was completing a program called the Forum, an intensive workshop which, at the time, lasted two weekends and an evening. She didn't know much more about it. I found out that my mother, a widow with very limited financial resources, had thrown all caution to the wind and flown from her home in North Carolina that day to join Jim for his final Forum session. She said she couldn't refuse—his enthusiasm was so contagious.

A few months later, my mother was back in New York taking the Forum and my sister was doing the same thing in Atlanta—at $650 a shot. (The structure and price of the Forum has since changed. It is currently one weekend and an evening, and the cost is $290.) I thought they were crazy.

I happened to be visiting New York the last evening of my mother's Forum and asked if I could come along—just out of curiosity, not because I was interested in doing anything so silly. Five minutes into the meeting, I saw why my family was so excited about this program. I wanted to find out more. I paid a deposit and enrolled. Two months later, in August 1988, I was in a hotel ballroom in Atlanta with about 100 other people, participating in the Forum.

That's how I discovered the world of Werner Erhard, the man who had designed the Forum and the program preceding that called The est Training.

My brother was right—my life has not been the same since.

I left the Forum with more questions than I had when I started, but I also had the sense that the answers—at least the kind of answers I had been looking for—wouldn't make any difference anyway. What was different was that a whole new world of possibilities had opened up for me. I saw that it was up to me to generate my own authentic answers to those difficult questions: "What's the meaning of life?" "What's my purpose?" "How can I combat rampant injustices?" and "How can I make the planet a better place?" I realized it was a mistake to look to someone else for THE answer—there was no such thing. It was exciting to discover that I had the tools I needed to deal with my own particular issues. All I had to do was put them to work—be intentional, committed, true to myself, and active.

Over the next three and a half years, I occasionally participated in various programs and courses offered by Werner Erhard and Associates (hereafter WE&A), particularly those dealing with communication. While I received tremendous professional and personal value from my participation, I always retained a healthy skepticism about the work, keeping my eyes and ears open for a "scam." In 1989 my editor asked me to write a series of feature articles about the work of Werner Erhard and my experiences. The stories were published in *The Macon Telegraph* in August 1989. Erhard had been too busy at the time for an interview, but for background information, I talked to people who worked with him and who had participated in his programs. I was surprised when I first approached the people in Erhard's San Francisco office at their apparent reluctance to answer my questions or help me get an interview with Erhard. I thought they would be thrilled to get publicity. Eventually I came to understand their hesitancy.

The first time I met Erhard in person was in December 1989 when he was in Atlanta leading a communications course. During one of the breaks, he requested to see me in private to thank me for the straightforward articles I had written. During that brief meeting, we discussed the general role of the media in shaping people's lives. He expressed his concern that what appears in the press as "the truth" often leaves people disempowered rather than informed. At the time, neither of us realized that Erhard soon would be destroyed by the media's version of "the truth."

Nearly two years later, we met again in September 1991. Erhard was staying at a friend's home in Puerto Vallarta, Mexico. His situation had changed drastically. He was no longer in the forefront of the personal growth movement. He had no place he called home, was no longer connected to the business to which he had given 20 years of his life, and his family had been torn asunder. He had gone into self-imposed exile just before he was publicly crucified in 21.8 million homes via CBS's March 3, 1991, *60 Minutes* program.[1]

Before that program, I had already seen some negative newspaper stories about him. One of the most disturbing was a long two-part series that came from the *San Jose Mercury News*, a large newspaper owned by the same Knight-Ridder Corporation which owned *The Macon Telegraph*. The Werner Erhard described by reporter John Hubner was entirely different from the man I knew and had heard about from others. I began to think maybe there was a scam, and that I had been duped by Erhard, whom I must have completely misjudged.

Whatever the case, I intended to find out. I started making phone calls to see what I could learn. There was obviously more to the story than what had been written in the San Jose paper. I was told that a group of former WE&A employees had axes to grind with Erhard and would stop at nothing to destroy him. I was also told that *60 Minutes* was in the process of preparing its own "expose," and the worst was yet to come. Because the war in the Persian Gulf dominated the news at the time, it took three months before the segment on Erhard finally aired.

In the meantime, a Houston businessman and close friend of Erhard's, Mark Kamin, had also been watching the negative publicity. Extremely intolerant of injustice, Kamin had long been supportive of social and political change. While working for a year as a free-lance writer for UPI in the Middle East, he had received a secret list of war criminals living in the United States. Kamin subsequently worked with Nazi hunter Charles Allen, who testified before Congress in 1976 in an effort to prod immigration services to prosecute war criminals in America.

Kamin felt certain that Erhard was not guilty as charged in the press. "What was in the media—the *San Jose Mercury News* and *The Marin Independent Journal* and then later *60 Minutes*—did not at all match my experience, nor the experience of thousands of people who had participated in Werner's programs. It just didn't ring true that the man who created these programs was the man portrayed in the press," Kamin said.[2]

He said he was well-acquainted with one of the senior *60 Minutes* producers, a man Kamin trusted and knew to be committed to the truth. Kamin had visited that producer in Paris in 1990, and while there, had dinner with him and others from *60 Minutes*, including executive producer Don Hewitt and senior correspondent Mike Wallace. Kamin said he sat across the table from Hewitt at dinner, and they talked throughout the evening. "Hewitt seemed to be a man of high values and integrity," Kamin said. "When the piece on Werner came out on *60 Minutes*, I was shocked. Here was an organization I respected saying things about a man that I couldn't believe were true. I was caught between a rock and a hard place."

In an attempt to resolve his conflict, Kamin called the producer of the segment on Erhard, David Gelber, the day after it aired. "I had seen quite a bit of evidence after the *San Jose Mercury News* article which proved that the article was inaccurate and I suspected that *60 Minutes* was also inaccurate, but wanted to hear what the producer had to say," Kamin said. To make sure he didn't miss anything Gelber said, Kamin taped the conversation, which Gelber requested to be confidential. Although Kamin has honored that agreement, he said that after listening to the tape several times, he became more convinced that something was not right. "I was left with this awful feeling of knowing how bad Werner had been wronged. However, I was bound by my word not to discuss my conversation with Gelber. I decided to do something about it," Kamin said.[2]

Having heard through the grapevine that I was asking questions about Erhard and the basis for the damning allegations, Kamin called me. He was looking for a hard-hitting, reputable investigative reporter who was willing to uncover and report the true story about Werner Erhard. He asked if I knew of anyone, making it clear that all he was interested in was the truth, not a coverup or defense. I didn't know of anyone but told him I would be glad to help

him find someone. We had several telephone conversations over the next few months as he continued
to probe into the allegations against Erhard. Every
time we talked, it became clearer this was a much
bigger story than had been publicized and there was
more behind it than just a few disgruntled former
employees.

In late August 1991, Kamin called and asked if I
was interested in taking on the project of uncovering that story. I immediately said yes, although he
warned me that I was basically on my own and that
it might even involve risking my life. He said he
would open the doors and provide whatever information he could for me, but I had to research and
piece the story together for myself.

Erhard had refused to speak with any member of
the press since the *San Jose Mercury News* articles
had appeared in November 1990, but Kamin was
able to arrange for me to interview Erhard. On a
warm September weekend, I met Erhard in Puerto
Vallarta.

Since leaving the country a week before the *60
Minutes* show, Erhard had been traveling all over
the world like a nomad. He had been to the Soviet
Union, Hong Kong, Japan, Europe, and Costa Rica.
He'd just recently arrived in Puerto Vallarta where
he would stay long enough to visit with friends and
family. Also while there, he was going to conduct
a seminar for a group of managers from the Soviet
Union who needed assistance in dealing with difficult situations in their turbulent homeland.

An informal dinner was scheduled the evening
before the interview, and a car was sent to pick me
up at the ocean-front hotel where I was staying. As
we maneuvered through the heavy traffic of the old
town, the friendly young driver told me about Puerto

Vallarta and how the movie *The Night of the Igua-
na* had changed it from a sleepy little town to a
major tourist attraction. I thought about the travel-
ers' guide in the hotel room which described the
town as a haven from the American rat race. I wondered if that was what brought Erhard here.

The multilevel house where Erhard was staying
was about the size of a small bed-and-breakfast inn
with private suites scattered around a central dining area, kitchen, and lobby. To one side, a veranda
overhung the cliff of a mountain on which the house
perched precariously. As we sat on the veranda
awaiting dinner, Erhard talked about his recent trip
to the Soviet Union and the work he'd been doing
there. The other six houseguests gradually emerged
from their rooms and joined the conversation. Some
were obviously just visiting, others were there to
work—to help Erhard prepare for the upcoming
seminar. As soon as everyone had arrived, we moved
into the dining area.

Erhard was clearly the center of attention at the
dinner table, but did not dominate the conversation.
When the discussion turned to religion and we were
recalling our childhood experiences, Erhard talked
some about the eight years he had been an acolyte
in the Episcopal church. I had forgotten that fact
which had been mentioned in his biography that I
read a few years earlier, but this image of him as a
10-year-old boy solemnly lighting candles in the
church was for some reason very touching.

After dinner, we watched a videotape of a live
concert by Liza Minelli and Sammy Davis Jr.that had
been filmed behind the scenes. Having met Sammy
Davis a few times before Davis' death, Erhard was
visibly moved by his ease and humor on screen,
speaking highly of him as the tape played.

The next morning, the atmosphere was different. While others worked, Erhard led me to the veranda for privacy. It was difficult not to be distracted by the majestic view of the ocean and the homes dotting the steep hillside, or by the sounds of the city far below. A gentle mountain breeze kept the heat and the bugs from becoming oppressive.

Still physically fit and of striking appearance, Erhard was relaxed but thoughtful as he began to talk about how he had gotten to this point. At no time during our long interview did he look, act, or speak like a 56-year-old man without a country, without a steady job, with a tarnished reputation and a family torn apart. His piercing blue eyes were intense as he gathered his thoughts to begin the intriguing saga of his life. The tape recorder on the small table at first seemed obtrusive, leaving little room for the ashtrays, notebooks, and coffee mugs, but we soon forgot it as Erhard began speaking.

For seven hours, I listened to an incredible story of espionage, conspiracy, and sabotage that sounded like it came right out of a best-selling spy novel. Erhard left no stones unturned, addressing every single allegation that had been made against him. The only thing he wouldn't talk about was his second wife, Ellen. Numerous newspaper articles have reported that a condition of their 1988 divorce settlement was that she could not talk about their marriage with anyone, especially members of the press.[3] He was either bound by the same agreement or felt that anything he said would be a violation of her privacy—he wouldn't say.

Finding his story almost unbelievable, yet entirely possible, I spent the next nine months checking it out. I made several trips across the country to study documents and to interview members of

Erhard's family, as well as former co-workers and friends. I also reviewed all the publications that had reported on him over the years, including his 1978 biography by the late philosopher, W.W. Bartley III, as well as reports on an organization that he said had done everything it could to orchestrate his downfall, the Church of Scientology.

The following story is about a man accused on national television of raping his daughter, physically abusing his children and wife, and being a greedy, power-crazed cult leader. This is also the story of a man who has devoted his life to making a difference for people all over the world, who was awarded the Mahatma Gandhi Humanitarian Award in 1988 for his leadership and "notable efforts to end the starvation and hunger suffered by millions each day,"[4] the same man who created and developed programs in which over a million people participated.

In addition to those people who have received value from Erhard's programs and those who have derived benefit from the various non-profit organizations he has helped make possible, there are others who have been deeply affected by Werner Erhard. People like Marie Harburger have serious cause for concern that Erhard is no longer in a position to make the kind of difference for others that he made for her.

Harburger, a psychotherapist in Wayland, Massachusetts, never took any of Erhard's courses and she never worked with him, but Erhard became a very important person in her life about four years ago. Harburger's brother, Jack Mantos, was Erhard's good friend and an executive in WE&A. In February 1988, while Erhard was on a boating vacation, Mantos died suddenly of a cardiac arrythmia. He was only 44 at the time and his death was a shock to everyone.[5]

Several of the negative newspaper articles appearing about Erhard in 1990 referred to that incident as pivotal in his organization for revealing the true cold-hearted nature of Erhard. Charlene Afremow, a Forum leader who was fired in April 1988, told *San Francisco Focus Magazine* that she was appalled when Erhard didn't show up for the funeral or memorial service for his friend. *Focus* reported that Mantos' wife had postponed the funeral twice waiting for Erhard to show.[6] Incensed at the magazine's lack of sensitivity and false reporting, Harburger wrote a letter to the magazine's owner, KQED television station.

"I do not know this woman (Charlene Afremow). There is nothing from this woman among our many touching gestures of condolence. She speaks of my brother and sensitivity, but she is a stranger to me," Harburger wrote. "This is ironic because the person who did step into my life in my grief was Werner Erhard."[7]

Harburger later told me that she had not known Erhard well before her brother's death and that the funeral had not been postponed waiting for him to return from the high seas. Mantos, who died on a Saturday evening in San Francisco, was returned to his family's home in Boston and buried there the following Thursday.[8]

"We held nothing up for Werner," Harburger said. "He was not a personal friend of ours. All we knew was that our beloved brother and son had died and our focus was on laying him to rest." Harburger said that as soon as Erhard returned to the country, he found her family. "He came to Boston, he called, he spent time with us." Harburger said that after the death of her brother, her father began to die also. He had spinal cancer and was ultimately paralyzed from the neck down.

"Werner stayed in touch constantly. I was never in the hospital with my father a day that Werner wasn't on the phone. They would end the phone call with Dad saying 'Goodbye, son.' The only other person in this world he ever said this to was Jack. He used to say 'Goodbye, son, I love you' at the end of every conversation, and Jack would say 'Goodbye, Dad.' Werner didn't know this, but I remember the first time it happened, my father said to Werner 'Goodby, son, I love you' and Werner said 'Goodbye, Dad.' It was so moving. My father was not confused, thinking he was talking to Jack. He knew exactly who he was talking to."

The night Harburger's father died, 18 months after her brother had died, she tried to reach Erhard and learned that he was leading an event in New York. "I tracked him down to the very room where he was. In fact, I could hear his voice in the background. Gonneke Spits (one of Erhard's long-time aides) answered the phone and I told her what had happened and requested that she wait until Werner was done before telling him. I knew he would be upset that my father had died. He called me first thing that next morning and thanked me for letting him do the event.

"He was thanking me for seeing him that way," Harburger explained. "I think that's the missing link in people getting mad at him. They invent him to be not human. He is a human being like other people—unique, but still human. And he deserves the same kind of respect for his feelings that he gives others.

"Werner stayed in touch even after that. He was the closest thing to my missing brother that I could ever hope for. I felt his support in every way. Everything was going fine. We were healing, he was there for us, and then all this stuff happened in his life.

"My gift to Werner right now is understanding that he can't be around. If I had known Jack was only going to have a 44-year life, I couldn't have asked for it to be any better. Werner gave Jack a forum on this planet for Jack to do what he most wanted to do, and I can't thank him enough for that."[9]

Regardless of what one decides about Werner Erhard, the public is entitled to know the whole story of who he is, something that *60 Minutes* and the publicity leading up to that program did not provide. Much of this book may be difficult to follow as is any complex conspiracy in which a human being is destroyed. To help the reader grasp the significance of the events treated in the following chapters and to understand how Werner Erhard had become so important that he became a threat to certain people, I have included an in-depth look at his accomplishments and the work that he created. I have also included an overview of the operations of the Church of Scientology.

[1] Nielsen Ratings, The Macon Telegraph, March 9, 1991.

[2] Interview with Mark Kamin, May 26, 1992.

[3] John Hubner, "Worlds of Werner," *West* of the *San Jose Mercury News*, November 18, 1990; Nikki Meredith, "Family Affairs: Werner Erhard's daughters tell of abusive father," *Marin Independent Journal*, January 6, 1991; David Gelman, Pamela Abramson, Elizabeth Ann Leonard, "The Sorrows of Werner," *Newsweek*, February 18, 1991; Elizabeth Fernandez, "Where is Werner Erhard? est guru leaves legacy of misery," *San Francisco Examiner*, April 21, 1991.

[4] "International Humanitarian Award Goes To You," *The Review*, newsletter published by Werner Erhard and Associates, January 1989, p. 9.

[5] Interview with Marie Harburger, June 21. 1992.

[6] Richard Rappaport, "Respect," *San Francisco Focus Magazine*, November 1980, pp. 81-84 and 138-142.

[7] Letter from Marie Mantos Harburger to Anthony S. Tiano, KQED, November 11, 1990.

[8] Interview with Marie Harburger, June 21, 1992.

[9] Interview with Marie Harburger, June 21, 1992.

CHAPTER II
SCIENTOLOGY DECLARES WAR

On December 29, 1991, nearly a year after Erhard's reputation was brutally destroyed on national television, investigative reporter and assistant city editor Robert W. Welkos revealed in a *Los Angeles Times* front-page story a shocking plot by the controversial Church of Scientology to put Erhard out of business. During Welkos' investigation, he discovered that church leaders had conducted an intense campaign against Erhard, using private investigators to dig up enough dirt to be fed to the media to crucify Erhard. Welkos reported that the campaign "would span more than a year and become one of the Church of Scientology's top priorities." This campaign culminated in an 18-minute segment on *60 Minutes* that destroyed Erhard's career. The evidence gathered by the *Times* and other sources showed that Scientology's use of the media to destroy Erhard actually started years earlier.[1]

In July 1977, the Federal Bureau of Investigation

confiscated thousands of documents in a raid of Scientology offices in Los Angeles and Washington, D.C. Among those documents were some showing that Scientology had been at work with the media against Erhard since the mid-1970s.[2]

The duration and intensity of the attack in the media by the Church of Scientology may explain how Erhard's record of creating programs and organizations that seem to have made a substantial contribution have instead been ignored and even distorted as something sinister. Each negative story about Erhard set the stage for the next one. The reporter doing his or her research pulled up an ever-increasing stack of negative stories as the basis for future articles.

Erhard had taken some Scientology programs during a brief period in 1969. Erhard told his biographer in 1978 that his practice over the years had been to explore a multitude of disciplines, and Scientology was one of hundreds in which he participated. Erhard said that he had found certain aspects of Scientology's characterization of Sigmund Freud's theory of mind interesting. The "reactive mind," as Scientology called it, is an extremely stupid stimulus-response mechanism that is run by its memory bank: by mental "pictures" from the past, including "engrams" (deep personal traumas that become moments of unconsciousness or pain). According to this characterization, every time a person encounters a new experience which reminds him in any way of an earlier trauma, the reactive mind causes the individual to automatically act as he had before, in a stimulus-response fashion. While Erhard found the theory interesting at the time, he rejected, among many other things, Scientology's idea of thetans. Thetans, according to Scientology, are immortal souls which accumulate the painful and traumatic experiences and pass on from one body to the next over trillions of years.[3]

After taking a few Scientology courses, Erhard went on to his next discipline and started working with Mind Dynamics in 1970. By that time he was already in the process of developing his own communications and training course,[4] but still checking out other disciplines and courses. Erhard would later learn that to start developing other programs after participating in the Church of Scientology's programs was a serious offense in the eyes of its founder and that by doing so, Erhard had begun to create a powerful enemy that ultimately would stop at nothing to destroy him.

Science fiction writer L. Ron Hubbard, who later founded the Church of Scientology, published a book in 1950 which he said he wrote in 30 days. In that book, *Dianetics: The Modern Science of Mental Health*, Hubbard claimed that he had discovered the source and cure for all kinds of human ailments. With dianetics, Hubbard professed to be able to restore withered limbs, mend broken bones, eliminate wrinkles, and increase intelligence.[5] The purpose of dianetics was to purge a person's "reactive mind" of the "engrams" which cause psychosomatic illnesses. According to Hubbard, once engrams are purged, an individual would be "clear" to fully function in life.[6]

Two years after publishing the book, Hubbard established Scientology as a religion aimed at "A civilization without insanity, without criminals and without war, where the able can prosper and honest beings can have rights, and where man is free to rise to greater heights."[7] He also took his dianetics theory a step further, saying that the only way to purge the accumulated engrams is through a long complicated process called "auditing."[8]

In 1971, the Church of Scientology issued an official order stating that Werner Erhard was expelled from the church because of "continued membership in a divergent group, namely, Mind Dynamics, Inc."[9] Hubbard was concerned, it seems with people taking his teachings and starting their own courses. He called people who did that "squirrels." [10] A 1990 six-part series of articles on the Church of Scientology in the *Los Angeles Times* described Hubbard's reaction in 1965 to a breakaway group. He ordered "his followers to 'tear up' the meetings of one such organization and 'harass these persons in any possible way.'"[11]

According to former church officials, Hubbard was furious with Erhard. He speculated that Erhard, who had started a new program of his own called the est Training, was using Scientology's teachings and would make millions of dollars that rightfully belonged to Hubbard.[12] The original order against Erhard was rescinded in a Scientology "Ethics Order" dated February 5, 1973, which said that Mind Dynamics was "not a divergent group, although Scientologists who stray from Scientology to join Mind Dynamics are diverging from Scientology." But that same order then declared that est was a suppressive group and that Erhard was guilty of treason.[13] Hubbard was never able to establish that Erhard used Scientology in his programs even though there was an all-out effort by Scientology lawyers to find a copyright infringement in Erhard's materials.[14]

A number of Scientologists have broken from the church over the years because of its heavy-handed tactics. Vicki Aznaran was one of them. She joined the Church of Scientology in 1972. A year later she went to work for the church, eventually becoming a manager in the "Commodore's Messenger Orga-

nization'' which executed Hubbard's directives.
Aznaran told the *Los Angeles Times* that in her official capacity with the church, when Scientology was
still trying to convince itself that Erhard had violated its copyright, she saw secret files that showed
Scientologists were instructed to enroll in est seminars, and that agents were planted in Erhard's office
to steal documents.[15]

Erhard explained why Scientology's efforts to
prove copyright violations failed. "It failed because
I was not using Scientology's material in my work.
All programs that deal with human beings will be
in some ways similar, if for no other reason, simply
because we all have minds and bodies, and we all
think and feel. In many significant ways, est was very
different from Scientology."[16] Scientology had to
resort to other means to get Erhard.

A 1990 book, *A Piece of Blue Sky*, sheds some
interesting light on how Scientology operates. The
book's author, Jon Atack, was formerly a member
of the Church of Scientology and is known today
as one of the world's foremost unofficial archivists
of the organization.[17]

"To the general public, Scientology was represented as a humanitarian, religious movement, intent
upon benefiting all mankind. Its opponents were
dangerous enemies of freedom, and were tarred with
unfashionable epithets such as communist, homo-
sexual, or drug addict. Opponents were portrayed
as members of a deliberate conspiracy to silence
Hubbard . . .," wrote Atack.[18]

"To its membership, Scientology was represented as a science, liberating man from all his disabili-
ties, and freeing in him undreamt abilities. To the
Church heirarchy, Scientology was the only hope
of freedom for mankind, and must be protected at
all costs."[19]

Atack wrote that Hubbard had a *Manual of Justice* which "laid down the law for Scientology staff members." This manual outlined a comprehensive "intelligence" and "investigation" system which provided the basis for Scientology's extensive use of private detectives to defame and harass its enemies.

"Hubbard certainly did not mind if the defamation was grossly exaggerated, or even a total fabrication. If you throw enough mud, some will stick," wrote Atack from his first-hand knowledge of church tactics.[20]

According to the 1990 *Los Angeles Times* series and Atack, Hubbard was also extremely paranoid about governmental agencies being out to "get" him and his organization. He was sure false information about him was being circulated around the world. The *Times* described a scheme by Scientology to purge government files of this so-called false information, an operation which turned into a huge criminal conspiracy by the church. As a result of the Church's actions, 11 of its leaders received prison terms, including Hubbard's wife, Mary Sue Hubbard.[21] According to the reports, Scientology spies "penetrated such high-security agencies as the Department of Justice and the Internal Revenue Service to find what they had on Hubbard and the church."[22] Perhaps not by coincidence, it was at the time Scientology agents were active inside the IRS that the IRS first became intensely interested in Werner Erhard. In the 1977 FBI raid of Scientology's headquarters, eavesdropping equipment and burglary tools were confiscated along with "48,000 documents detailing countless operations against 'enemies' in public and private life."[23] The secret Scientology documents the FBI gained in the raid on Scientology's offices contained several references to

Scientology's campaign to harass and discredit Erhard.[24]

By the time Aznaran left the church in 1987, she was overseeing the Office of Special Affairs which had previously been called the Guardian's Office. This was the arm of Scientology which was responsible for enforcing its "fair game" policy. Aznaran said that policy gave Scientologists free rein for harassing any perceived enemy of the church without fear of being disciplined for their actions. In other words, anyone declared "fair game" is subject to being tricked, sued, stolen from, lied about, and destroyed. Erhard was declared fair game by Scientology in 1973 and was therefore targeted for destruction.[25]

In a 1982 interview with *Penthouse*, Hubbard's son, L. Ron Hubbard Jr., who had left the church in 1959, described how Scientology's enemies were treated, especially those who attempted to write unfavorably about the organization. "First, they'd try throwing every possible lawsuit at the reporter or newspaper. We had a team of attorneys to do just that. The goal was to destroy the enemy. So the solution was always to attack, full-bore, with every possible resource, from every angle, instantaneously . . . . A guy would get slapped with twenty-seven lawsuits and our lawyers would start deposing absolutely anybody who ever knew the man, digging up dirt while at the same time putting together an operation that would get him into further trouble."[26]

Paulette Cooper was one of the unfortunate writers who found out to what levels Scientology would go in its attack on those who, like Erhard, were declared "fair game." In the summer of 1971 she published a critical book about the church, *The Scandal of Scientology*. According to Hubbard Jr., Scientology spent a half a million dollars trying to

destroy her[27] and almost did. The lawsuits started
first. Cooper and her publisher were sued separate-
ly in several U.S. and foreign cities until the publisher
finally withdrew the book. After receiving anonymous death threats and discovering her telephone
was being tapped, Cooper filed a $15.4 million law-
suit against Scientology for harassment. A few
months later, she was indicted by a grand jury for
sending bomb threats to the Scientology office. It
was not until almost a year after being indicted that
the authorities were finally willing to believe her
protestations of innocence when she passed a sodi-
um pentothal lie detection test. The actual source
of the bomb threat, however, was not known until
the FBI raid of Scientology's headquarters uncovered
internal documents showing that Scientology had
surreptitiously obtained Cooper's fingerprints on a
blank envelope from her apartment. They then used
that envelope to mail to themselves the anonymous
bomb threat which they had written, all in a scheme
to frame Cooper and have her incarcerated in a mental institution or jail.[28]

While viewing some of the seized Scientology
documents after they became public in late 1979,
Cooper came across an est internal document which
she subsequently sent to Erhard with a note saying
she assumed it was stolen from his office. She
informed Erhard she had seen other documents
indicating that Scientology had taken actions to
expose criminal activities and, toward that end, had
planted Scientology members in his office.[29]

To this day, despite the massive campaign mount-
ed to uncover anything that would hurt Erhard, no
evidence has ever been found linking him to anything criminal, nor has he ever been indicted for a
crime, despite the impression in recent articles that
he fled the country to avoid prosecution by federal

authorities in his current tax cases.

Given that Erhard could not be stopped by criminal or civil prosecution, Scientology operatives wove allegations together in the media such that a picture of Erhard could be formed that would destroy his public image. This was accomplished by feeding them to a press that had been primed over time. Ultimately, the media provided the kangaroo court in which the mere making of the allegations was enough not only to convict, but to eliminate Erhard.

The Church felt protected in its dealings with the media by an aggressive policy of litigation that made them less susceptible to being attacked while they worked on Erhard and other "enemies." L. Ron Hubbard Jr. told *Penthouse*, "My father drilled into all of us: Don't go to court thinking to win a lawsuit. You go to court to harass, to delay, to exhaust the enemy financially, physically, mentally. You file every motion you can think of and you just lock them up in court. The courts, for my father, were never used to seek justice or redress, but to destroy the people he thought were enemies."[30] According to Aznaran, Scientology has a three-million-dollar annual budget just for private investigators and attorneys.[31]

In an ironic twist, Scientology had apparently tried to take certain material Erhard had invented before they put into effect their "final solution" of using the media to exterminate him. Aznaran told the *Los Angeles Times* in December 1991 that Hubbard was very jealous of and angered by Erhard's success. Aznaran said Hubbard's followers tried to duplicate est's success with a plan run by one of Hubbard's daughters which involved sending "lots of people into est and copying it." But they were never able to make Erhard's methods work for them.[32]

In the epilogue of his book on Scientology, *A Piece of Blue Sky*, Jon Atack wrote "The Church is a very rich and a very dangerous organization. There is no indication that it will change its ways. Hubbard's policy is now considered 'scripture,' and according to Scientology Policy Directive 19, of 7 July 1982, Hubbard alone can alter these 'scriptures.'"[33] While Hubbard is now dead, his words declaring that Erhard was fair game live on as scripture, not to be altered by logic or common sense.

Scientology demonstrated that it is indeed rich. When *Time* magazine published a May 6, 1991, expose of the Church of Scientology, the Church launched an avalanche of paid media. It ran full page ads in *USA Today* multiple times per week and a 28-page glossy insert called "The Story That TIME Couldn't Tell," which explained and defended the organization's philosophy.

A review of the 1992 revision of the book, *L. Ron Hubbard Messiah or Madman?*, by the *Vancouver Sun*, said "The fright created by a Stephen King horror novel can be quickly laughed off. But this highly unauthorized biography of the founder of Scientology creates a weirder than fiction chill that won't go away."[34]

Erhard did not seem frightened or despondent during my interview with him. "I am clear that Scientology considers me its enemy," Erhard said, "and perhaps will not stop in its efforts until I no longer exist, literally. But that is their problem, and I don't choose to make it my own. Of course, I will take whatever steps I need to take to be prudent about protecting myself from them. But I will not let it interfere with living.

"They made their contribution to the recent

changes in my life, but after all, changes are only changes. One day it's like this, and the next day it's like that. No one can take away a person's self-respect, except the person him- or herself."

Erhard has never been overly concerned or dependent on what others think of him. "For many years I have made a distinction between self-respect, reputation and image," he said. "Self-respect is a matter of relating to yourself based on your own actions. Like everyone else, I sometimes have bad thoughts and sometimes my reactions are bad, but finally I see myself based on my actions. It is easy to fake sincerity, but you can't fake action. You either did or you didn't and that's all. It's not a matter of judging or evaluating yourself.

"I use the word reputation to mean how those who have personal, direct knowledge of you have experienced your actions personally. Have they been enlivened and empowered in their direct experiences with you? When they needed counsel or support, did your actions make any difference to them?" Erhard said he knows his use of reputation is not the usual interpretation of the word, but he thinks it's important to distinguish between how he's seen by those who have no real direct experience of him, and those who do have direct experience. "My actions, my way of being with them personally, did or did not make a contribution to their life. Through the programs I've led, and the other work I've done in the world, I have had the privilege in the last 20 years of being unusually close to a very large number of people. With the vast majority of those people, using that definition of reputation, I have a very good reputation," he said.

"As to image, how one is held by those who have merely heard about you, or whose view of you at the moment ignores their direct experience of you and is primarily predicated on what they have been told by others, for this phenomenon—what I call image—I have little concern. The media has seen to it from the very beginning that I never had much of an image. And for the most part, that didn't stop me from fulfilling the opportunities people gave me to make a contribution.''

Erhard said he sees no value in striking back at those who have tried to harm him. He's much more interested in what he can contribute to others, an opportunity he views as a privilege, than how much damage he can do. ''If that turns out to shorten my life, or to deprive me of certain possibilities, that is the price I will have to pay for living a life the quality of which is determined by my own choices about how I will be in life. I have given up resentment and regret as being follies because ultimately they produce no good for anyone,'' Erhard said.

''Scientology and those engaged in the web it has spun can do no harm to what is precious to me. I might wish the circumstances had turned out otherwise, but that too is folly. Where one set of possibilities is cut off, I do whatever I can to restore them, and in whatever room is left after that effort, I create new possibilities and go on.''[35]

It's not only journalists, critical writers, or Erhard who have been targeted as ''fair game'' by Scientology, but attorneys as well. Boston attorney Michael Flynn became interested in the activities of Scientology in 1979 when a former Scientologist retained him to get her money back. Not long after Flynn took that case, someone put water in the gas tank of his plane almost causing a serious accident. He suspected Scientology was involved.[36] As Flynn took on more clients with complaints against Scientology, he soon became an expert on the organization and was asked in 1982 to help the city of Clearwater, Florida, investigate the Church's activities.[37] According to Atack, Flynn fought against the Church for seven years, spending a lot of his own money and often putting his career in jeopardy.[38]

"In a surprise move in December 1986, the Church settled every case brought against them through Boston attorney Michael Flynn," wrote Atack. "In a secret agreement, the plaintiffs agreed not to make any further public statements about Scientology, nor to disclose the amount of their settlements. . . . Scientologists bought the silence of their most significant opponents." Flynn subsequently turned over his files to the Church.[39]

Former WE&A officials claim that before Flynn was silenced by the settlement, he came across some shocking information about the lengths to which Scientology might go to destroy Erhard. In an internal memo to Erhard dated March 30, 1983, WE&A counsel Art Schreiber wrote: "I took a call today from Michael Flynn . . . who stated that one person has informed him (Flynn) that such person was involved in having a contract put out on your life several years ago, and that there was evidence which would corroborate the fact that such action was taken. Flynn said that given the serious nature of this matter, he wanted to notify us of this. Flynn stated that once he received the evidence, he would have to turn it over to the FBI. I said that we would very much like to see the information to determine if we should go to the FBI or bring legal action against Scientology." Schreiber said that Flynn agreed to provide that evidence once he received it and ensured that his client was protected.[40]

A second memo from Schreiber to Erhard, dated June 2, 1983, said: "I called Flynn again today and spoke with him. He said that he was awaiting authorization from the person to release the information. Flynn said he received a tape from the person containing the information and that he prepared a written affidavit setting forth such information. . . . Flynn volunteered that the person said some 'pretty amazing things,' . . . Flynn also said the person currently is in 'semi-hiding' and he could not be sure when he will hear from him regarding the permission (to turn over the evidence that Scientology had put a contract out on Erhard's life)."[41]

No "smoking gun" regarding the alleged plot on Erhard's life has ever been seen. Flynn maintained his silence after the 1986 settlement with the Church of Scientology and never got back to Schreiber. Whether the threat was true or not, two of Erhard's outside attorneys took the possibility of such a threat against Erhard seriously. They recommended that he remain out of the country when he left on a trip for the Soviet Union in 1991. One of Erhard's attorneys wrote to him on August 2, 1991: "I do believe that you are under the very real threat of physical and legal harm. . . . It is easy for those of us having grown up in a civilized society to think that thugs and hit men only happen in the movies. . . . Recent articles about your enemies suggest that they would not be above such tactics."[42] One of Erhard's remaining close associates who has stayed in touch with him during Erhard's self-imposed exile, said that the concerns for Werner's safety had a lot to do with Erhard becoming so inaccessible to people since his departure.

Hubbard hated Erhard and was determined to destroy him, a mission which was passed on to his successors in the scriptures he left them after his death in 1986. In 1989, Scientology found a new opportunity and its attack on Erhard took on renewed vigor. A wrongful termination suit filed against Erhard and his company by a former employee in December 1988 provided that opportunity. At least three private investigators were hired as agents so that Scientology could remain in the shadows in a new campaign against Erhard. They were told to find out or "dig up" damaging information about Erhard and launch a media campaign to destroy his reputation. But until recently, they never admitted to any of those they spoke to that they were working for Scientology. Two of those investigators, Ted Heisig and Alan Clow, went on record for the December 1991 *Los Angeles Times* article which uncovered Scientology's campaign to discredit Erhard. The third, Seth Derish, would not talk with the *Times*.[43]

Ted Heisig, a private investigator in Orange County, California, told the *Times* that when he was hired in October 1989 by Scientology to investigate Erhard, he was shown five file cabinets filled with documents on Erhard that dated back to 1943. The *Times* stated that it was clear to Heisig from the beginning that "Scientology was preparing a 'media blitz' against Erhard—and that he was going to be a key player, spreading and collecting information that could be used to discredit the est founder."[44]

Heisig's orders were to do "legal checks on Erhard to see if there were criminal cases lodged against him, contact disaffected former est employees and members and conduct surveillance of Erhard's boat." While the Scientology agents never found evidence of anything criminal, and the constant, long-term surveillance of the boat on which he lived revealed nothing, Heisig said he interviewed several dozen people with instructions to get information on Erhard's "questionable activities" and to "persuade people with such knowledge to file sworn affidavits against Erhard."[45]

Alan Clow, a private investigator in Newport

Beach, said he was hired by Scientology to investigate "Erhard's background and the relationship with his daughters"—to dig up dirt. He talked to an estimated 20-30 people. Heisig said the third investigator, Seth Derish, who refused to talk to the *Times*, was instructed to obtain "financial information on Erhard and his organization." Heisig said he saw the reports that Derish submitted.[46]

Both Clow and Heisig said they were instrumental—directly or indirectly—in feeding allegations to journalists around the country under the direction of Scientology. Their efforts started the negative media publicity in 1990 which culminated in the nationally televised show on *60 Minutes*. Scientology operative, Alan Clow, admitted to the *Times* that he had fed material to the producers of the *60 Minutes* segment that destroyed Erhard.[47]

When Scientology sent out its agents in 1989, there were two separate lawsuits pending against WE&A, neither of which had received much publicity. The plaintiffs of these two lawsuits didn't know about each other. One was the wrongful termination suit by Charlene Afremow and the other was a damage suit by former program participant Paul Gutfreund.

Scientology instructed its investigators to exchange information with these plaintiffs who were suing Erhard and put them in contact with each other.[48] Things really started heating up after that.

[1] Robert W. Welkos, "Scientologists Ran Campaign to Discredit Erhard, Detective Says," *Los Angeles Times*, December 29, 1991.

[2] "Scientologist Plot Revealed," *The Denver Post*, November 25, 1979.

[3] W.W. Bartley III, *Werner Erhard: The Transformation of a Man; The Founding of est*, (New York: Potter), 1978, pp.149-154.

[4] Bartley, p. 158.

[5] L. Ron Hubbard, *Dianetics: The Modern Science of Mental Health*, (Los Angeles: Bridge Publications), 1950; Robert W. Welkos and Joel Sappel, "The Scientology Story: A Special Report," *Los Angeles Times*, June 24-29, 1990.

[6] Welkos and Sappel, *Los Angeles Times*, June 24-29, 1990; Bartley, pp. 152-153.

[7] "The Story That TIME Couldn't Tell," published as a public service by the Church of Scientology International, 1991. Insert with full-page advertisements in *USA Today*.

[8] Welkos and Sappel, *Los Angeles Times*, June 24-29, 1990; Jon Atack, *A Piece of Blue Sky*, (New York: Carol Publishing Group), 1990, pp.131-136.

[9] Internal Scientology memo addressed to Those concerned from Ethics SFO, February 5, 1973, "HCO Ethics Order," referring to Cancellation of EO #366:SFO dated June 22, 1971.

[10] Atack, p. 38.

[11] Welkos and Sappel, *Los Angeles Times*, June 24-29, 1990.

[12] Welkos, *Los Angeles Times*, December 29, 1991.

[13] Internal Scientology memo, February 5, 1973.

[14] Welkos, *Los Angeles Times*, December 29, 1991.

[16] Welkos, *Los Angeles Times*, December 29, 1991.

[16] Interview with Werner Erhard, September 15, 1991.

[17] Atack, p. vii.

[18] Atack, p. 143.

[19] Atack, p. 143.

[20] Atack, pp. 143-145.

[21] Welkos and Sappel, *Los Angeles Times*, June 24-29, 1990; Atack, pp. 226-241; Bent Corydon, *L. Ron Hubbard: Messiah or Madman?*, (New Jersey: Barricade Books Inc.), revised edition, 1992, pp. 156-171.

[22] Welkos and Sappel, *Los Angeles Times*, June 24-29, 1990.

[23] Welkos and Sappel, *Los Angeles Times*, June 24-29, 1990.

[24] *The Denver Post*, November 25, 1979.

[25] Harry Rosenberg affidavit, reference Vicki Aznaran.

[26] "*Penthouse* interview with L. Ron Hubbard Jr." *Penthouse*, 1982, pp. 111-113 and 166-175.

[27] *Penthouse* interview, 1982, p. 112.

[28] "Author of a Book on Scientology Tells of Her 8 Years of Torment," *New York Times*, January 22, 1979.

[29] Undated letter to Werner Erhard from Paulette Cooper.

[30] *Penthouse* interview, 1982, p. 112.

[31] Harry Rosenberg affidavit, reference Vicki Aznaran.

[32] Welkos, *Los Angeles Times*, December 29, 1991.

[33] Atack, pp. 397-398.

[34] Corydon, 1992, back cover.

[35] Interview with Werner Erhard, September 15, 1991.

[36] Atack, p. 273; Corydon, p. 239.

[37] Atack, p. 273.

[38] Atack, p. 357.

[39] Atack, p. 357.

[40] Internal WE&A memo to Werner Erhard from Art Schreiber, March 30, 1983.

[41] Internal WE&A memo to Werner Erhard from Art Schreiber, June 2, 1983.

[42] Letter to Werner Erhard from attorney, August 2, 1991.

[43] Welkos, *Los Angeles Times*, December 29, 1991.

[44] Welkos, *Los Angeles Times*, December 29, 1991.

[45] Welkos, *Los Angeles Times*, December 29, 1991.

[46] Welkos, *Los Angeles Times*, December 29, 1991.

[47] Welkos, *Los Angeles Times*, December 29, 1991.

[48] Welkos, *Los Angeles Times*, December 29, 1991; Sworn affidavit by Ted Heisig, October 29, 1991.

CHAPTER III
A WEB IS WOVEN

In March 1988, Paul Gutfreund filed a civil lawsuit against Erhard and various entities and individuals with whom Erhard was associated. Gutfreund's suit alleged that he was mentally damaged from participating in several courses designed by Erhard and that a charity with which Erhard was related had taken advantage of him. In December 1988, Charlene Afremow filed a $2 million civil lawsuit against Erhard, his company, and one of its executives alleging that she was wrongfully terminated from the company in April 1988 because of sex and age discrimination.

The actions taken by these two litigants and one of their lawyers would result in a massive guilty verdict for Erhard, not one handed down by a jury or a court, but one handed down by the media. Scientology would achieve its victory over Erhard.

Art Schreiber was the general legal counsel of Werner Erhard and Associates (WE&A) when both of these suits were filed. He explained how the two plaintiffs, who had no knowledge of each other's suits, started working together after Scientology got involved.

"An investigator for Scientology, Ted Heisig, came to San Francisco in late 1989 with instructions to obtain damaging information on Werner and the organization for use by Scientology. As it turned out, Heisig discovered that there were two pending lawsuits in San Francisco against Werner and WE&A, and Scientology apparently determined they could damage Werner by supporting these lawsuits behind the scenes rather than taking direct action against him. Heisig's actions brought the two litigants together and supported both of them. Heisig gave Gutfreund names of people to interview regarding damaging information about Werner, and Gutfreund gave Heisig names of other people to contact for damaging information. Heisig fed Gutfruend information and documents on Werner from Scientology, and Gutfreund fed information and extensive documentation on Werner and the organization to Heisig. In fact, Heisig told Gutfreund about the Afremow lawsuit, and Gutfreund then contacted Randy Loftin, Afremow's long-time boyfriend, in early 1990. From that point on, Gutfreund and Loftin exchanged documents, tapes, and names of potential witnesses to support their common purpose of damaging Werner and the organization. Scientology reaped the benefits of the Gutfreund-Afremow actions without having to take direct action."[1]

Charlene Afremow had been Erhard's instructor when he participated in the Mind Dynamics course in 1970. Then in 1975, she went to work for him as an *est* Trainer Candidate—someone who was being trained to lead the *est* course.[2] When the *est*

Training was retired in 1984 and replaced by a new program Erhard had developed called the Forum, Afremow became a Forum Leader Candidate.

In April 1988, at a monthly public meeting of Forum Leaders, company policies regarding the Forum Leaders' out-of-town travel were being discussed. Afremow stood up and announced that she was not going to comply with those policies because she felt they were too difficult. Consequently, she was fired by Steve Zaffron, a WE&A executive in charge of the Forum Leaders, for refusing to follow policy.[3]

Laurel Scheaf, another Forum Leader Candidate who led the Forum, said it was almost as if Afremow came to that meeting with the premeditated intention of forcing Zaffron to fire her. "The limits on travel and numbers of days worked in a month policies being discussed were no different than they had always been. In fact, the meeting was really about not working more than those policies allowed. But Charlene said in front of everybody that she wasn't going to do it," said Scheaf. "She already worked less and traveled less than the limits the policy set. Management had accommodated her request for a personally less demanding schedule. But Charlene attacked Steve and flatly refused to comply with the company's policy. In fact, it was she who gave Steve the alternative of firing her. As an executive of the company, Steve had no choice when given this public ultimatum but to fire her. By the way, Werner wasn't even there, he had nothing to do with it and didn't know it was happening."[4]

As Afremow left, she announced that they would be hearing from her attorneys. The company did hear from Afremow in the form of a complaint which she filed with the California Department of Fair Employment and Housing. The agency determined that

Afremow's complaint lacked merit and took no action against WE&A.[5]

Afremow then found an attorney who apparently thought that even though the State of California found her complaint without merit, he could win money by filing a suit against Erhard and WE&A. Not long after Afremow's attorney, Andrew Wilson, filed the lawsuit, Schreiber (WE&A's in-house legal counsel) said he began receiving telephone calls from people—current and former employees—saying that they had been contacted in relation to the Afremow case and were asked by the caller to say damaging things about Erhard.

Karen Gerbosi, who had left WE&A in 1987 after 15 years of working with Erhard, said in a sworn affidavit that she was contacted by another former employee of the company who told Gerbosi that she was working for Afremow. The caller told Gerbosi they were looking for people they could get involved in the lawsuit against WE&A. A month later, Wendy Drucker, another former employee, called Gerbosi and said that she was working as a volunteer paralegal for Afremow's attorney. She told Gerbosi she was contacting people trying to do something about the "wrongs" Erhard had done to them and other staff members. Gerbosi told Wendy she had nothing bad to say about Erhard and had actually enjoyed working with him.[6]

Gerbosi said that she heard from several other former colleagues that they too had been contacted by Wendy or her husband, Vincent Drucker. "One former colleague said Vincent Drucker said 'This was a once in a lifetime opportunity to get in on the ground floor to destroy Werner Erhard,'" Gerbosi said.[7] The Druckers made numerous calls to former employees of WE&A looking for those with a grudge against the company. At first, these calls were apparently made at random, but as they went on, one disaffected employee knew of another who was disaffected. Utilizing this networking technique, the Druckers were able to gather a small group of disaffected ex-employees out of the hundreds of former employees of the 20-year-old international program. They were only able to find 10 former employees willing to blast Erhard and his company, but that was enough to do the damage they set out to do.[8]

Vincent Drucker started working with Erhard in the late 1970s as the chief financial officer for *est, an educational corporation (est, a.e.c.)*. His wife, Wendy, assisted with some of the programs and events and occasionally held various jobs in the company. While they were both on staff, they had a fairly close working relationship with Erhard.

Schreiber said that, "given the incredible support Werner had provided for the Druckers, their actions against him were reprehensible." He then recounted the tragic circumstances of the Druckers' 2-year-old baby drowning while they were on an outing in Yosemite in the late 1970s. "The first person they called from Yosemite was Werner. Werner told them to come on back, 'I'll be here for you.' They came back to San Francisco and met with Werner for hours and hours. He supported them with his time, his care and his love, and also provided other people to support them. I clearly remember that I was participating in an *est* seminar in Washington, D.C., and my seminar director read us a letter from Wendy Drucker expressing her deepest appreciation to Werner and the *est* staff and organization for their profound contribution to her and Vincent during this tragic period, without which support they didn't know if they would have retained their sanity."[9]

Gonneke Spits, one of Erhard's aides who had worked with him since the mid-1960s, was working with Erhard when the Druckers returned to San Francisco from Yosemite. "We sat with them in the study at the Franklin House [where Erhard lived and had his office at the time] and went through their agony. What had happened to them was really horrible. He was so wonderful with them and took care of them. Years later, he even helped them sort out their relationship when it was going sour," Spits said. She said she has no idea why they turned against him, but they obviously decided he was an evil man who must be destroyed.[10]

It wasn't until Schreiber and others received reports about the Druckers' telephone calls that anyone knew the Druckers had a grudge against Erhard. Vincent Drucker left the employ of *est, a.e.c.* Reportedly he had an interest in the chief executive officer's position with the company and didn't get that job. His wife stayed as a volunteer and occasional employee for a few years after that.

Erhard said that he had almost no contact with them after they left the company. "Wendy volunteered her services for a short time and Vincent did some consulting for a partnership I had with another man, so they were apparently still my friends at that time. I didn't see them at all during the years after that and I have no idea what would cause them to turn on me so viciously," Erhard said.

"When we worked together, I supported each of them as fully as I could. They had the kind of tragedy in their family that leaves deep scars. We went through that together. At first when we met right after the accident, they were blaming the child's death on their neglect. I worked with them until they could see that what had happened was an accident, not their fault. The guilt, the grief, the sense that life has been irreparably maimed, all of it took a long time to get resolved," Erhard said. About a year later

the Druckers announced they were having another
baby. "When the baby came, it was a daughter. The
new baby was like a gift, not to replace the daughter they lost, but to fill the hole her absence made,"
Erhard said. He also said when he later worked with
the Druckers on saving their marriage, he admired
them for how they handled it.

"Vincent and Wendy had always been people who
thought for themselves. When we worked together, Vincent often had views about the business that
were different than mine. He was generally forth-
right about those views. I respected him for his independence of thought and his no-nonsense approach
to business. Even on those occasions when we disagreed, I respected his ideas and he always acted like
he respected mine. After he left the company, he still
liked what I was doing well enough to accept my
offer to consult on resolving an issue with my part-
ner in a software company."

Erhard said he doesn't understand why the Druck
ers turned on him. "My only explanation for their
unexpected attack is that they rewrote the history
of our relationship and somehow found in that
rewritten history a reason to hate me for what I had
been in their lives."[11]

Tirzah Cohen, who worked with Erhard for 17
years, has a different interpretation of what may
have happened with the Druckers. Cohen said that
there was nothing like working closely with Erhard,
and when people left staff, there was a vacuum. She
compared the experience to being on a basketball
team. "When you were in the game, Werner's relationship with you was that you were part of the
team. There was a certain camaraderie, a certain
team spirit. Your life is different when you leave the
team, no matter how good your friendship was with
those people or how great the camaraderie, that

team is still going on. It's a different team now because you're not on it. Those remaining on the team might still be great friends with you, might call you from time to time, but are not available to be with you as much as they would like to.

"That's sometimes how life is and that's very much what it was like when people were here [on staff]," Cohen said. "They had a particular relationship with Werner and then they left. No problem with them leaving, but when they weren't part of the game any longer, which is what his life is about and he doesn't do things that aren't part of what his life is about, it wasn't the same—it couldn't be the same. Except people wanted it to be the same. They wanted to have the same benefits, the same contribution, the same outcomes, and the same relationship with him that they had when they were playing the game full out. When that didn't happen, it could often be an occasion to make somebody wrong."[12]

Substantiated by their correspondence with Erhard and their actions while still on staff, the Druckers clearly at one time valued Erhard's friendship and support. But the situation was different when they were no longer working closely with him, and they obviously resented it.

Wendy volunteered paralegal services to Afremow's attorney and loaned Afremow $5,000.[13] Vincent and Wendy Drucker became involved early in the Afremow case and played a major role in sifting through hundreds of former employees to find those few who were willing to make damaging allegations against Erhard. They were gathering complaints to make the case that working conditions at WE&A were horrible and oppressive, that Erhard was abusive with his employees, and that Erhard was eccentric and excessive in his personal life. Almost nothing they got the people who attacked Erhard to say had anything to do with wrongful termination. But apparently, the legally irrelevant allegations made against Erhard were very important to Wilson's plan to extract money from WE&A.

Another major player in the web being woven against Erhard was Landon Carter. Carter took the *est* Training in 1972 and soon after joined the staff where he eventually became a Trainer, head of the business and finance department, and a member of the board of directors. A few years later, Carter met his future wife Becky in a seminar he was leading. Erhard was best man at their wedding for which he also paid.[14]

Erhard said that Carter was eventually fired when he refused to not participate in the Iditarod, an annual 1,100 mile grueling dog sled race in Alaska from Anchorage to Nome. The staff at the Iditarod headquarters in Wasilla, Alaska, remember Carter from the 1980 event. One woman said in a telephone interview that she recalled that Carter never even got to the first 10-mile mark. At the beginning of the race, one of his dogs fell and was dragged by the rest of the dog team. The staff member explained that once a dog goes down, it takes so long to stop the rest of the 14-to-18 dog team that the fallen dog is usually dragged to its death. Although she couldn't remember the specific coverage about Carter, she said the press always covers dogs being killed in the races. Because Carter's dog was down so early in the race, it's death probably got even bigger coverage than usual.[15]

"Landon was enthralled by the whole idea of the Iditarod," Erhard said. "But I asked him not to participate because I didn't think he was prepared. The agreement between the trainers and myself at that time was that they would do what I asked them to do. There were times trainers did not keep that

agreement and usually that was fine when I saw that
I made a mistake in what I asked or at least that they
had made their best effort. In this case, the chance
of damage to the dogs and maybe even to Landon
was too great, so I fired him. As it turned out, in spite
of my warnings, he did compete and one of his dogs
died. Those reporting on the race blamed his inex-
perience and lack of preparation."[16]

Scheaf, who had worked with Erhard even before
he started the *est* training, was a colleague of Carter's. "He became a star when he was in charge of
the 6-Day course [one of Erhard's programs designed
to help people break through the barriers in life] and
started loving the power. He developed the attitude
that he knew better than anyone else, including
Werner," said Scheaf.[17]

"One of my jobs at *est, a.e.c.*, was to train,
develop and be responsible for the people who led
the *est* Training—the Trainers," Erhard said. "Their
training and development was very demanding and
arduous and it usually spanned many years. Taking
on becoming an *est* Trainer was not something anyone should have entered into lightly."Erhard said
that Trainers were told from the beginning about the
demands that would be made on them and that they
would be expected to forego the kind of rights com-
monly enjoyed by other employees. "As always, in
spite of our great effort to make it clear beforehand,
there were people who didn't really grasp what the
experience would be like. These people weeded
themselves out very early in the program," Erhard
said.

"One aspect of the training these people received
was much like a long Marine boot camp and officer
candidate school rolled into one. The idea was to
transcend the personality people had developed as
adolescents and modified as adults, so that they were

free of the limiting aspects of ego and personality. We had learned in working with people over the years that even the personality traits which were useful in the successes they had produced in life were ultimately limiting when they became something on which the person was dependent for success. Rather than being free to express themselves through these successful personality traits, they were limited to them." Since one of the requirements for becoming Trainer Candidates was that people already be successful in life. Erhard said they consequently had lots of these personality traits to transcend.

"The end result was a person not constrained by their ego or personality when conducting the course and who was truly free to express themself fully. Virtually everyone who got designated as a full-fledged Trainer had achieved a remarkable transformation in themself. They knew what it is to live life both with the constraints and limiting memories all of us develop and to be free of those constraints and limits. Before their training was over, they had a profound compassion for the quirks, limits, and distortions produced by bad experiences, and even for the egos of the people who participated in the programs that they led," said Erhard.[18]

Erhard talked about what sometimes became a problem for the trainers. "The trainers' compassion, power, and unrelenting commitment to what people could be was obvious to those who participated in the programs they led. They were respected, admired and often loved by the people they trained. That was when the advanced part of their training began," Erhard said.

"What happened is that instead of lightly accepting the admiration, respect, love, and support they received, the trainers would become too engrossed in it, almost enamored of it or attached to it. When trainers took their attention off what produced that response from people and began to attend to the response itself, invariably their ability to produce results in people's lives suffered." Erhard said the Trainers referred to that as tripping over the wall they called "going for the goodies."

"I think that may be what happened to Landon," Erhard said. "Landon was one of those remarkable people. As an *est* Trainer, he had produced awesome results in thousands of people's lives. He was admired, loved and supported by literally thousands of people. The people he had trained in Alaska provided the opportunity for him to experience driving a dog sled. As the outstanding athlete he was, I'm sure he loved that experience. But I think Landon tripped over the wall. I think the Iditarod was a case of Landon going for the goodies with the people who loved and respected him."

Erhard said that he also loved, admired and respected Carter and hated having to fire him. "I know that making the contribution he was able to make in people's lives was enormously rewarding and fulfilling for Landon. I'm sure he was painfully torn between that fulfillment and whatever he was looking to get out of participating in the Iditarod. I told him that while he could choose to stay with the company as an executive and participate in the Iditarod, he couldn't participate and continue to be a Trainer. I think he made a mistake in the decision he made and it took him years to forgive me for that mistake."

Several years later, Erhard said he recommended Carter to Ted Turner, who was looking for somebody to head a new charitable foundation he was forming. "Since I never lost my respect and regard for Landon, and because I thought he had the qualifications for the job, I recommended him. Ted ultimately offered the director's job to someone else, but offered Landon a very good job with the foundation which Landon accepted," Erhard said.

After Carter left *est*, Erhard said he wrote to him occasionally suggesting they get together and resolve their differences. "Sometime after Landon went to work for Ted's foundation, he took me up on the latest of those offers. We got together in New York City in my hotel room. I apologized to Landon for anything I had done in that situation many years ago that might have made the decision he had to make even more difficult for him. We updated each other on our lives, and forgave each other for anything we had done to each other. We hugged, and Landon left with a smile on his face, and left me feeling good as well for having completed together something that had been incomplete for so long," Erhard said.[19]

Carter was first approached in November 1989 by one of the private investigators hired by Scientology to find people disaffected with Erhard. At that time, Carter told the investigator, Ted Heisig, that he had nothing bad about Erhard to say. Carter was approached again in January 1990 by Alan Clow, another Scientology investigator, and told him the same thing.[20] However, soon after that, Carter was drawn into the web the Druckers were spinning.

Both Carter and his wife were quoted extensively by John Hubner in a series of articles in the *San Jose Mercury News* in November 1990, talking about how oppressive Erhard was in their lives. They said horrible things about their former associate and teacher. Although he obviously felt quite differently during the many years he worked with Erhard, among other things, Landon Carter told the reporter that the only reason Erhard started *est* was to make money, the driving force behind everything he did.[21]

The damning allegations in the declarations and affidavits gathered for Afremow's wrongful termination suit painted an ugly picture of Erhard. But they contained almost nothing legally relevant or permissible as evidence in a trial for wrongful termination. Perhaps Afremow and her attorney had a strategy that included conducting the trial in the press. Could Erhard stand to have these allegations come to light, or would he settle the case he had every reason to believe he could win, just to avoid having these unfounded yet brutal allegations against him made public?

The judge hearing motions in the case expressed his displeasure at Wilson's conduct of trying the case in the media and admonished Wilson not to do that. Undeterred, Wilson filed declarations from several individuals hostile to Erhard which contained the damning allegations against Erhard, ostensibly as evidence in the case. The judge ordered these declarations to be placed under seal and not made part of the public record. Apparently the judge felt Erhard was entitled to the protection of the court against just what finally happened—brutal allegations against Erhard made public in the media which were never subjected to proof of any kind nor against which Erhard would ever be permitted to defend himself.

According to Schreiber the judge later acted to sanction Wilson for his conduct in filing these declarations. The judge issued an order in which he stated that these declarations contained material which was "scandalous, salacious, defamatory and devoid of relevance". Given this, the judge found that these declarations were filed in bad faith and ordered that Wilson pay Erhard sanctions in the amount of $1,500. Art Schreiber stated that "the fact that an award of sanctions against an attorney is highly unusual in this court is clear evidence that the court considered that Wilson's action calculated to damage Erhard was well beyond the bounds of responsible conduct.''

Despite the knowledge of the court ordered seal, the media loved the sensationalism of the devastating allegations made about Erhard by his ex-employees in these declarations and published many of them. If Afremow's attorney did in fact hope to wring a healthy cash settlement out of Erhard by feeding the allegations to the press, he must have been licking his chops at the job the press was doing on Erhard. The media might make it unnecessary to win a trial on legitimate grounds. Art Schreiber said that in his opinion, this was how Wilson intentionally conducted the case all along. "He knew his case was weak, so he used the media to create an environment to force Werner to settle out of court," Schreiber said. In addition, Schreiber stated that, ''Wilson's commitment to use the media to further his strategy was also evidenced by his highly unusual appearance on a radio talk show in San Francisco to discuss the case and repeat the unfounded allegations against Werner.''[22]

Erhard's response to these allegations was short. He said, ''they are simply untrue.'' However, those making the allegations against Erhard needed to have no concern that they would ever be required to prove the truth of what they said in destroying Erhard's reputation. Erhard was defenseless against the massive attack on him. He had no choice but to just take it.

In a strange legal quirk, the law itself rendered Erhard defenseless. The law protected his attackers from any retribution, from being sued for giving false witness, or for slander or libel. Anything said in a lawsuit is protected. Nor would those making the vicious allegations being used to paint Erhard as a truly immoral man ever need to worry about the truth of the allegations they made. The allegations, all of which were made in support of pretrial motions, would never be subject to proof because the judge ruled that they were irrelevant and, therefore, would not be admissible in the trial.

By the time these documents were filed, Afremow and the other litigant against Erhard, Paul Gutfreund, had already joined forces and were collaborating against Erhard. Obviously, Afremow and those working with her kept Gutfreund informed of their actions. They let him know just when they would be filing particular documents—which might explain how Gutfreund happened to go to the court and get copies of the documents before the judge had a chance to order them sealed. Gutfreund promptly took the documents to reporter Don Lattin at the *San Francisco Chronicle* and, it is assumed, distributed them to other members of the press who Gutfreund knew had an interest in Erhard. Ted Heisig said in his sworn affidavit that Gutfreund was in "regular and sometimes daily conversation with Lattin." Heisig also said that the Afremow documents Gutfreund gave Heisig did not have the court stamp on them, indicating that Gutfreund had obtained them from a source other than the court.[23]

Paul Gutfreund had filed his personal injury suit against Erhard and his company around the same time Afremow was fired. Gutfreund, a former engineer, had participated in several courses offered by Erhard over a seven-year period. He was actively involved in The Hunger Project, the non-profit organization founded by Erhard in 1977, and donated large sums of money and many volunteer hours. In his lawsuit, which included The Hunger Project,

Gutfreund claimed that his participation caused him mental suffering and suicidal behavior.

Prior to filing his lawsuit, Gutfreund had a dispute with The Hunger Project and tried to get back a donation he had made. The organization informed him that as a non-profit, it was not allowed to refund contributions. After that, he started his full-time vendetta against Erhard. Gutfreund devoted his time to spying on Erhard and his staff and amassing boxes of files on him and the organization. He stole documents from WE&A, altered them or took them out of context and sent them out anonymously to various members of the press, attorneys, anti-cult groups and others. He told Ted Heisig, and anyone else who would listen, that Erhard was a neo-Nazi in the 1970s and extremely dangerous to society and that The Hunger Project was a CIA front.[24]

During discovery in his lawsuit, Gutfreund admitted being under psychiatric care and on lithium, an anti-depressant, to maintain his mental stability. He also admitted sending out anonymous packages to various journalists around the country containing damaging information on Erhard. His attorneys told the court on more than one occasion that Gutfreund was unavailable because he failed to take his lithium and that left him unable to function normally. Greg Gillen and Lou Kraushaar, Internal Revenue Service agents Gutfreund was trying to interest in Erhard's activities, wrote in a memo to IRS District Counsel in Sacramento on March 27, 1991, that Gutfreund had earlier threatened to commit suicide if the IRS proceeded with actions to collect a delinquent tax liability from him.[25]

Perhaps Gutfreund himself knew that he had no real grounds for a case against Erhard. His actions indicate that he was delusional about Erhard, hated Erhard and wanted to see him destroyed, but that is not grounds for a legitimate lawsuit against someone. Four years after filing his suit against Erhard, the judge finally dismissed Gutfreund's case against Erhard on the basis that although he was repeatedly ordered to provide the court and the defendant with the grounds for his claims, he never did so. In this case also, the judge found it necessary to censure and fine the plaintiff's side for using underhanded tactics against Erhard. At the time the case against him was dismissed, the court awarded Erhard a judgment against his antagonist, Paul Gutfreund.

Gutfreund was included with the Druckers, the Carters and the others involved in the cases against Erhard who were being interviewed and quoted as experts on Erhard and his work by several Bay Area newspapers and journals including the *Marin County Independent Journal, San Francisco Focus Magazine, San Francisco Examiner, San Francisco Chronicle,* and the *San Jose Mercury News.* In many cases, only portions of the declarations were quoted in these periodicals. People who had positive experiences to report on Erhard and his work were rarely interviewed and when they were, even more rarely quoted.

While the court wound up throwing Gutfreund's case out, he was taken very seriously by the Bay Area media. They frequently quoted him in relation to the Afremow case as well as his own case and used him as a major source for their reporting on Erhard. The media's source of information on Erhard was this man who by his own admission was sick, needed to medicate himself just to stay functional, and was, on the evidence of his actions, delusional about Erhard. While the media made much ado about Paul Gutfreund's case against Werner Erhard, when the court dismissed the case as groundless, the media was silent. As of this date, there has been no mention of the dismissal of the case which the media had so widely publicized.

Besides the damage the three Scientology agents got Gutfreund and the disaffected former employees to do for them, their crafting of the matter was further revealed during depositions taken for the Afremow case. It was discovered that Afremow had at least two direct contacts with Scientology marked on her personal calendar even though in direct questioning during her deposition, she denied ever having met with Scientology. Afremow's boyfriend said that he introduced Afremow to a Scientologist who was an old Army buddy of his, and others in Scientology. Randy Loftin, her boyfriend, said they were interested in Afremow's feelings about Erhard.[26]

One cannot help but notice the similarities in the tactics used by Afremow's attorney against Erhard, and the tactics for abusing the courts espoused by L. Ron Hubbard, Scientology's founder. Wilson's connection to Scientology during the Afremow case was evidenced when he hired one of the three Scientology agents, Seth Derish, to act for him as a private investigator in Afremow's case. According to the *California Bar Magazine,* by March 1992— after Afremow's trial was over—Wilson was working directly for the Church of Scientology as legal counsel, representing the church in several lawsuits. Responding to a reporter's speculations about Wilson's apparent connections to Scientology, Wilson replied he considered Scientology "to be a valued client, and they'll get the best that I can do."[27]

In April 1991, a jury found no basis for Afremow's claims of wrongful termination nor any evidence of sex and age discrimination against her by WE&A. Although she had asked for $2 million, the only judgment the court awarded her was $28,400 because it found that the company had hindered her from starting her own competitive course on relationships after she was fired.

Erhard's victory in this case got scant notice in the press. If it was mentioned, it usually got the headline that Afremow received an award in her case against Erhard, not mentioning that she had obviously consumed at least a half a million dollars in attorney's time and other costs and expenses. The press never noted that the allegations that defamed Werner Erhard, and which they had enjoyed sensationalizing, had not been proven.

[1] Interview with Art Schreiber, December 31, 1991.

[2] Bartley, p. 173.

[3] Interview with Art Schreiber, December 31, 1991; Interview with Laurel Scheaf, June 8, 1992; Interview with Werner Erhard, September 15, 1991.

[4] Interview with Laurel Scheaf, June 8, 1992.

[5] Interview with Art Schreiber, December 31, 1991.

[6] Sworn affidavit by Karen Gerbosi, December 25, 1990.

[7] Sworn affidavit by Karen Gerbosi, December 25, 1990.

[8] Interview with Art Schreiber, December 31, 1991.

[9] Interview with Art Schreiber, December 31, 1991.

[10] Interview with Gonneke Spits, June 5, 1992.

[11] Interview with Werner Erhard, September 15, 1991.

[12] Interview with Tirzah Cohen, June 5, 1992.

[13] Deposition of Charlene Afremow, Charlene Afremow v. Werner Erhard, et al.

[14] Interview with Werner Erhard, September 15, 1991.

[15] Interview with staff member at Iditarod headquarters in Wasilla, Alaska, June 5, 1992.

[16] Interview with Werner Erhard, September 15, 1991.

[17] Interview with Laurel Scheaf, June 8, 1992.

[18] Interview with Laurel Scheaf, June 8, 1992.

[19] Interview with Werner Erhard, September 15, 1991.

[20] Sworn affidavit by Ted Heisig, October 29, 1991; sworn affidavit by Harry Rosenberg, May 23, 1992.

[21] John Hubner, "Worlds of Werner," *West* of the *San Jose Mercury News*, November 11, 1990.

[22] Interview with Art Schreiber, December 31, 1991.

[23] Sworn affidavit by Ted Heisig, October 29, 1991.

[24] Sworn affidavit by Ted Heisig, October 29, 1991; Interview with Art Schreiber, December 31, 1991; Interview with Werner Erhard, September 15, 1991.

[25] Internal IRS memo to District Counsel, Sacramento District from Greg Gillen and Lou Kraushaar, March 27, 1991.

[26] Henry Rosenberg affidavit, reference Afremow v. Erhard et al.

[27] Steven Pressman, "Mixing Lawyers and Cults," *California Bar Magazine*, June 1992, pp. 22 and 24.

CHAPTER IV
THE STAKES INCREASE

In May 1991 John Hubner, reporter at the *San Jose Mercury News*, was awarded top honors for investigative journalism by the Sunday Magazine Editors Association for his "expose" on Erhard which appeared as a two-part series in the *News'* Sunday magazine, *West*, in November 1990.[1]

Hubner's series fully exploited the negative material on Erhard generated in the Afremow case, which the San Francisco press had already made so abundantly available.

It used the allegations made by the ex-employees connected with the Afremow case, the material gathered by Paul Gutfreund, and interviews with the Druckers and the Carters. But the articles were new in two ways. Firstly, Hubner skillfully put all the available negative material into one published piece which produced a searing highly believable portrait of Erhard that mocked his public record. Secondly, for the first time, however, there were damning allegations made against Erhard by a member of his family.

What the Editors Association did not know when they made that award was that Hubner's scoop of the first allegations by a family member came from a daughter, Celeste Erhard, who had been battling a drug problem for years. Also she had been heavily pressured by her mother, Erhard's ex-wife, Ellen Erhard, to turn against her father. "The truth is that I was turned against my father with lies and clever manipulation. I was ripe to be exploited, and that's exactly what happened," Celeste said.[2] The balance of the new allegations regarding Erhard's relationship with his family came from a former governess for the Erhard children. This woman, now a close friend of Erhard's ex-wife, had been working closely for over a year with one of the agents hired by Scientology to destroy Erhard.[3]

The awarding editors also did not know that Hubner induced Erhard's daughter, Celeste Erhard, to make the damning allegations against her father by offering her a book deal which he told her, in his opinion, could result in payments of up to one million dollars. "John Hubner, working with Dawn Damas, my mother's former housekeeper, induced me with promises of vast sums in which I would share, so that I made up things that were not true about my father, corroborated what I knew to be lies of others and, finally, never made it clear when I knew something that someone said was false. Over the weeks, John Hubner kept insisting that he needed sensational material and that I needed to 'beef up' my story for there to be a market for the book he and I would write. He said he expected a million dollar contract and that I would receive half, if not more, of the profits."[4]

Unbelievably, Hubner himself had unwittingly

provided documentary evidence of the deal he offered Celeste. This only came to light when Celeste later recanted and began to repair the damage she had done. She said that she had been induced by Hubner to lie, exaggerate the truth, and falsely corroborate unsubstantiated allegations made by others. Celeste explained that she had insisted Hubner at least put something in writing to evidence the deal he made with her. The letter John Hubner wrote to Celeste Erhard, dated October 10, 1990—a month before his award-winning "expose" was printed—read in part: "I will send the finished articles to my agent, Robert Gottlieb, vice-president of the books division at the William Morris Agency in New York City. Were a book project to develop, you, Celeste, would be a major part of it and I would share the advance and any royalties the book earned with you in a fair and equitable way that we were both happy with."[5]

The Editor's Association also didn't know that Celeste, when she began to see the damage the lies about her father had wrought, specifically told Hubner that some of the things she had said for his article were outright fabrications. Celeste and her husband, Christian Santangelo, independently said that Hubner's response to the news that his articles about Erhard contained lies, was to just blow it off with a flip of the hand and the comment "That doesn't matter."[6]

Scientology showed its hand in Hubner's articles when it came to light that his other source of allegations about Erhard's relationship with his family, Dawn Damas, was working with Scientology. Damas had become close friends with Erhard's ex-wife, Ellen, during the Erhards' bitter divorce in 1988.

While Erhard and his ex-wife may have been constrained by their divorce agreement from defaming each other, Damas spoke without such compunction. According to Scientology agent Heisig's sworn statement, Damas told him a hair-raising story about Erhard's relationship with his ex-wife and their three children. Heisig said that he had the "feeling everything Dawn told me was coming straight from Erhard's former wife."[7]

In fact, Dave Rios, Erhard's former son-in-law, said in a signed affidavit that he overheard several conversations between Ellen Erhard and others about how she was going to get Erhard. One particular conversation between Ellen Erhard and Damas, while Damas was working with Heisig, stood out in Rios' mind. He said that he overheard Ellen tell Damas that she appreciated what Damas was doing "more than you can imagine, and I will take care of you in many ways."[8]

After years of effort which only resulted in harassing Erhard, Scientology was rewarded with what they needed for the final solution. They could now feed the media what was necessary to destroy Werner Erhard's life. They could fulfill L. Ron Hubbard scriptures because Dawn Damas provided access to the most intimate and sacred area of the man's life, his family.

Ellen Erhard, from all appearances Erhard's other greatest enemy, had in the Damas-Scientology relationship what she previously lacked to be effective in her reported obsession to destroy Erhard. Scientology knew how to use the stories about Erhard that she had reportedly been telling her children and her friends for many years but without the desired effect. Apparently while Scientology needed what Ellen Erhard could provide, Ellen Erhard needed what Scientology could provide to accomplish the objective they both shared. Although there's no direct evidence linking Ellen Erhard with

Scientology, Damas connected the two in their mutual hatred of Erhard. The web around Erhard was complete, in that Ellen Erhard also had ready access to the four children of Erhard's first marriage. Werner himself provided that access, and Ellen used it to tell her stories to the rest of his children.

The members of Erhard's family report that during Erhard's divorce, even before the possible constraint of the settlement agreement, Werner Erhard never spoke derogatorily about Ellen and encouraged the members of his family to maintain their personal relationship with her. Celeste told me, "My father never said anything negative about my mother. In fact, whenever I told him that my mother and I had argued, he always encouraged me to give up any resentment toward my mother and reconcile with her."[9] Without knowing it, Erhard was strengthening the access his ex-wife had to each of his seven children.

Celeste, a very outspoken young woman who minces no words, told me about her dilemma. "I cannot emphasize enough that my whole reality was not my own, but my mother's. It became 'Us'—me, Mom, St. John, Adair—against Dad. I was told things like 'If your father found out about this, he would get very pissed off and violent, so it's a good thing I know so that nothing will be said to him and you won't get hurt.' Of course, there were many vivid stories about what went on when I wasn't around, even when it wasn't true, which I believe was the case now. I eventually became frightened of Dad. At the time, I didn't realize that these feelings had no basis in reality, because I only had one reality— Mom's."[10]

Although Celeste was 27 when we talked, she said she had only recently realized what was going on. "Over the years I had been worked on so that history had been rewritten for me, and I had been instilled with a negative perspective toward my father. When I stood on my own two feet and looked for myself, when I relied on my own experience and my own judgement, I realized that my father had been good to me and I couldn't remember a single time that he dealt with me or any of his children, motivated by his own needs.''

While there is also no evidence that Ellen Erhard ever spoke directly to John Hubner, Damas once again provided the connection necessary for the achievement of Ellen Erhard's and Scientology's mutual objective. Soon after Damas' discussions with Scientology's Heisig, she started working with John Hubner. It was Damas who first talked Celeste into speaking with Hubner, using a dream Celeste had always had for enticement.Although she looks like she could be a rock star—like her father, Celeste is very striking—she said she was interested in writing. Celeste had wanted to write a book about her family since her college days when she was majoring in literature. She thought it would make an interesting story because it was such an unusual and unique family. She also loved to write and loved books.

"Years before any of this happened with John [Hubner], I had told my mom I wanted to write a book. I just wanted to write about Dad and the family, how it felt to be in that family. You know, the whole me generation thing. I asked her please not to tell anybody because it would just start a big deal and plus, I don't want anybody to take my idea," Celeste said. "So the next thing I know, we're at a surprise birthday party for my mom at Lucille's, my mom's best friend, and Dawn was there. Lucille and all those other people there were all Mom's Sweet Adeline buddies, her singing group. Dawn was always invited, but she never showed up. But she's there this time and next thing I know, she comes up to me and says 'I hear you want to write a book about your dad?' And I said 'Where did you hear this from?' I told her I didn't say it was specifically about him and I told her what I wanted it to be about. She said 'Listen, I know somebody who's doing that exact thing right now.'" Damas told Celeste that John Hubner was working on a book about her father and it would be a perfect opportunity for her to get her story out, possibly writing the book with Hubner.

"I thought 'this is going to be the best I get'," Celeste said. "I thought I might as well go meet this guy because he's already starting to write this thing. And I can't compete with an author. She didn't even tell me he was a reporter. In fact, when he said 'I'm just going to tape this for the article,' I was surprised. I had no idea."

Celeste said she asked him what books he had written that she might have read. "He said, 'Well, I've actually only written one book about Hare Krishnas, but right now I'm working for the *San Jose Mercury News*. I'm a reporter.' He made it sound as if it was a temporary job. I should have said 'Look, I was lied to, you're not who you said you were. And I don't want to do this.' But, of course, I didn't." Hubner told her he expected and needed to publish the articles first in the newspaper to generate an interest in the book.[11]

At the time, Celeste was in serious financial straits. She had just placed herself in a drug-rehabilitation program and was struggling to recover from a brutal addiction to painkillers that she had developed after a car accident years earlier. She was in counseling and beginning to sort out her relationship with her family, but still in the initial phases. Damas and

Hubner were both fully aware of Celeste's state of mind but encouraged her to talk poorly of her father anyway.

Celeste said that Damas was present at all of her interviews with Hubner. She was prompted to make damaging allegations that Celeste knew weren't true or at least had no knowledge of. Celeste felt like Hubner wasn't interested in anything positive she had to say about her father. "He just asked me sleazoid questions like 'I've heard that your dad sticks his hands up women's skirts when they waitress for him, is that true?' I said 'Well I don't know about that, I've never seen that.' He really asked only *National Enquirer* kinds of questions."

Hubner told Celeste that after his articles came out, maybe they could appear on the "Geraldo" show on TV and get more publicity for their book. "Well, it turned out to be *60 Minutes* instead of 'Geraldo'," Celeste said, "but the same idea."[12]

Celeste added that Hubner kept pushing her to "beef up" her story. "I would answer 'I don't know' or 'I don't want to talk about that kind of stuff.' He'd say, 'Well you're going to have to do better than that if you want a book to sell. People aren't going to be interested. Be creative.' He didn't outright say 'lie,' but he definitely said 'You're going to have to be more creative than that; you have to have a better answer than that.'

In his articles, Hubner printed allegations that Damas made about Erhard beating his 12-year-old son, St. John, for making bad grades and about Erhard choking and beating his wife at a family meeting in 1977, after which she was supposedly banned from the family except as a maid, neither of which were true. Hubner also printed tales Damas told him about late-night orgies that Erhard held and made his ex-wife participate in, tales that Damas had gotten straight from Ellen about which no one who worked closely with Erhard had any knowledge. Hubner quoted Celeste at length as she laid out a very believable tale about Erhard keeping guns and drugs on his boat, a lie Celeste said he had suggested to her and which she and her husband later told him was untrue.

After Hubner's series, Celeste's younger sister, Adair Erhard, started talking with reporters from other Bay Area publications. Celeste said that Adair hadn't talked with Hubner because at first she didn't want to jeopardize the money she was receiving from her father at the time. But, according to Celeste, Adair was encouraged by their mother to get involved in the attack on Erhard and soon changed her mind. Celeste also said her mother promised to take care of Adair financially so she wouldn't need any more money from her father. Celeste said Adair didn't remember any details about the events that reporters were asking her about so she asked Celeste to tell her what to say. "I told her everything I had been saying, including the lies, so she could act like she knew what she was talking about."

Hubner played a major role in interesting the people at *60 Minutes* in doing a story on Erhard, and he and Damas paved the way for the Erhard daughters to appear on the show. Celeste explained what happened. "Supposedly John worked something out to interest '60 Minutes.' He didn't say what. All he would say was partly they got interested because of his article, but that he also called them to try to get them to do something on it. He wouldn't say any details or anything. But Dawn was the one who introduced us to Gelber (David Gelber was the main producer of the *60 Minutes* program that was aired on Erhard)."[13]

Although Hubner claimed to be writing a book on Erhard, one might question the intention behind the claim. Instead of writing a book on Erhard, shortly after his articles were published he was engaged in writing another book. But whatever his motives, he clearly played a role beyond that of a reporter only interested in publishing the truth. After his articles were written, he went on to provide the opportunity for the final solution.

[1] "About Awards," *Editor and Publisher,* May 18, 1991.

[2] Interview with Celeste Erhard, February 22, 1992.

[3] Sworn affidavit by Ted Heisig, October 29, 1991.

[4] Interview with Celeste Erhard, February 22, 1992.

[5] Letter to Celeste Erhard from John Hubner, October 10, 1990.

[6] Interview with Celeste Erhard, February 22, 1992; Interview with Christian Santangelo, February 23, 1992.

[7] Sworn affidavit by Ted Heisig, October 29, 1991.

[8] Sworn affidavit by Dave Rios, February 21, 1992.

[9] Interview with Celeste Erhard, February 22, 1992.

[10] Interview with Celeste Erhard, February 22, 1992.

[11] Interview with Celeste Erhard, February 22, 1992.

[12] Interview with Celeste Erhard, February 22, 1992.

[13] Interview with Celeste Erhard, February 22, 1992.

CHAPTER V
60 MINUTES JOINS THE GAME

When John Hubner, the San Jose Mercury News reporter, approached *60 Minutes* to interest them in telling the Erhard story on national television, they had already been primed by a packet of material on Erhard from another member of the web, Paul Gutfreund. Each of the groups in the web out to destroy Erhard were now fully connected to each other.

Scientology was connected to each of the elements of the web. It was directly connected to Gutfreund; to Afremow and the group of individuals the Druckers had gathered around her; and through her friend Dawn Damas, effectively connected to Ellen Erhard, and the children she was inducing to join her against her ex-husband; and connected to the members of the press writing about Erhard. Scientology sometimes gave its input for the stories directly to the reporter, and sometimes got its input to the press through Gutfreund, Damas, the Druckers, or one of the individuals the Druckers had gathered together.

The Afremow group, which included Charlene herself, her boyfriend Randy Loftin, Wendy and Vincent Drucker, and the group of disaffected ex-employees they had gathered, were also effectively connected to all the other elements of the web around Erhard. They were directly connected not only to Paul Gutfreund and Scientology, but directly connected to Ellen Erhard. Celeste reported that she had been with her mother when her mother met with Afremow and Loftin on two occasions during the period when the Afremow case was a great source of allegations against Erhard.

The Afremow group also had full access to the press through no less than three avenues: either by direct contact with the press; or, until the judge censored them through Afremow's attorneys; and the final avenue, Paul Gutfreund, who provided the media with the documents which the court had sealed. Afremow failed to force Erhard into a settlement through the media attack on his reputation and eventually lost the case she hoped to win in trial. Immediately after the jury's verdict was announced, Afremow's boyfriend Loftin delivered a message to Lynn Erhard, who was present at the trial in her father's place. Loftin said, "You can tell your father from me, this isn't over yet."

Erhard's ex-wife, Ellen Erhard, was also connected to each of the other elements in the web. The connection that would in the end prove deadly to Erhard and destroy his reputation was that between Ellen Erhard and the children who served as her mouthpiece. While her confidante, Dawn Damas, guided their actions, Ellen Erhard, who had schooled Erhard's children in hatred toward their father, spoke from the shadows. Adair Erhard told interviewer Ed Bradley that her mother was thankful for what she was saying on the *60 Minutes* show about Werner Erhard.[1] Adair, like her sister, had a history of substance abuse. She was a single mother and totally dependent on Ellen Erhard for support, and like her sister, the perfect weapon to be used against Erhard. Scientology was getting what it wanted through the web of hatred connecting Erhard's enemies.

Members of the press reporting on Erhard had reason to suspect that the people they used had a powerful vendetta against him. It was clear that the people they were quoting were corroborating each other's stories. Each had their own individual version, but all painted one consistent picture of Erhard. It was unmistakable that they were people well connected to each other and with a common motive.

Although the producers of *60 Minutes* had strong reason to believe that the notorious Church of Scientology was out to destroy Erhard and was the impetus behind the negative press, the producers apparently chose to ignore that information. Anthony Pellicano, a highly respected Los Angeles private investigator, told me that he had been hired on more than one occasion by *60 Minutes* in some of its investigative pieces. On that basis one could assume that he was known to the producers to be highly credible and extremely thorough in his work.

Pellicano, who has been featured in numerous articles and television programs, said that he talked many times to Ted Heisig while Heisig was employed by the Church of Scientology. Pellicano had been retained by Erhard's people to find out why private investigators were suddenly so interested in Erhard's business, asking questions of his co-workers and former colleagues. After finding out what Heisig was up to, Pellicano stated, ''I was compelled to intercede in what I knew to be an undeserved, national

media smear campaign against Erhard. I was aware
that the *60 Minutes* television program was planning
a piece using the allegations that Scientology had
already been successful in getting published in the
print media and which I knew to be highly suspect
if not outright lies."[2]

Well before the show was aired, Pellicano called
60 Minutes producer, David Gelber. "I informed
him that there was a conspiracy to destroy Werner
Erhard," Pellicano said. "I told him that Scientology was using Paul Gutfreund, Wendy and Vincent
Drucker, and Charlene Afremow to do their dirty
work. I said that Gutfreund, with the help of Scientology, had gotten the stories, filled with false allegations, into the media."

Pellicano also said he told Gelber that Dawn
Damas and three of Erhard's children were unwit-
ting dupes of Scientology and that the children were
getting back at their father. "I told Gelber that he
was wrong, dead wrong, and I couldn't have been
clearer that he needed to do further research into
the allegations he was preparing to broadcast over
national television." Pellicano said that Gelber
thought he had enough information and that his
sources were reliable, despite what Pellicano was
telling him.

60 Minutes had already been enticed into producing a segment on Erhard while Hubner was working on his articles for the *San Jose Mercury News*.
One of the three Scientology agents, private investigator Alan Clow, told the *Los Angeles Times* that
he provided *60 Minutes* information that he had
"dug up" on Erhard.[3] Hubner told Celeste that he
contacted CBS about doing something on Erhard;[4]
Paul Gutfreund, the disaffected participant, told Heisig that he contacted *60 Minutes*.[5] A *Village Voice*
columnist wrote in January 1991 that Jesse Korn-

bluth, long-time Erhard foe, had run into trouble getting an article he had written on Erhard published in *Vanity Fair* or *New York* magazine, so consequently had sold his material to *60 Minutes.*[6] One of the Scientology agents later stated that Kornbluth had been fed some of that material by Roger Stodola, the person in the San Francisco Scientology office designated to operate the local campaign against Erhard.[7]

David Gelber, the *60 Minutes* producer assigned to create the show's segment on Erhard, had an initial lunch meeting with William E. Barnes of Erhard's public relations firm, Barnes and Clarke. He was attempting to persuade Barnes to allow him to interview Erhard. He later wrote Barnes on November 9, 1990, that he intended to produce an "important story about a fascinating man" and that he was interested in "shedding some light on the new phases of his work— rather than simply concentrating on his past."[8]

It didn't take Barnes or Erhard long to figure out that Gelber was misrepresenting his intentions and that *60 Minutes* was, in fact, not putting together a story on Erhard's work at all. Until the very end, Gelber attempted to mislead them. Gelber maintained the lie until San Francisco's gossip columnist Herb Caen wrote, "It's open season on Werner Erhard, who must be wondering what hit the fan and why. Bloodied by nasty stories in *San Francisco Focus* and the *San Jose Mercury News,* he will next be savaged on *60 Minutes,* whose Ed Bradley arrives today to begin preliminary work. You know, like sharpening the long knives."[9]

Even though Gelber's letter appeared very sincere and though he gave his personal assurances that he intended nothing but a balanced piece, Erhard's people knew that what he said was inconsistent with the facts. Gelber was interviewing none of the many thousands of people whose only story about Erhard, his work, and organizations was that they enjoyed great benefits. In fact, but for two possible exceptions, he was not even interviewing people who could respond to the allegations. Instead, Gelber and his co-producer, Doug Hamilton, were interviewing, those former employees and other individuals who had already made public allegations against Erhard.

In the letter to Barnes, Gelber had said, "We think it's in everyone's interest that we speak with people who are in a position to respond to allegations against him and his associates. We're pleased that you'll help us with those contacts, and, of course, we're especially eager to talk with Werner."[10]

While Gelber was given a long list of people who had personal, direct evidence that the allegations that had been published against Erhard were false, he actually spoke to almost no one on the list and didn't bother to tape even one of them for possible use on the show he was putting together. Further, two of the daughters who did appear on the show later said that *60 Minutes* had edited out of their interview all positive comments they had made about their father.[11]

It's possible that David Gelber may have had other influences. The court record in Chicago regarding a suit Erhard filed against CBS and David Gelber, which is discussed in a later chapter, alleged that "on information and belief," Gelber and Damas were having an affair.[12] Celeste said that Damas confided in her that Gelber and she were lovers. Celeste's husband, Christian Santangelo, also said he felt strongly that this was true.[13] When reached for comment, Gelber said he couldn't speak about this on the record without consulting CBS attorneys who were not available. Damas never returned my phone calls. No other information is available to confirm or deny the allegation at this time. However, Gelber spoke with me extensively off the record. Regardless of the veracity of the allegation regarding he and Damas, it's my opinion that his production of the CBS program on Erhard was at least flawed and unprofessional.

As legal counsel and one of the senior executives of Erhard's business, Art Schreiber early on made himself available to be interviewed by *60 Minutes* about various business activities of WE&A. He wanted to be sure that the producers had accurate information about Erhard and the organization.

"I was interviewed, but not on camera, by David Gelber," Schreiber said. "At the outset, he tried very hard to convince me that he wanted this to be a fair and balanced piece. However, I quickly got the sense that this was a preconceived hatchet job waiting to happen. I met with him for an hour and a half and gave him lots of facts about the organization and about the work. I told him that if he really wanted to do a fair and balanced piece, and he wanted to say all these things they printed in the *San Jose Mercury News*, why didn't he say 'here is a man about whom they say these things" and also that 'here is a man who did the following: Created the Forum and other programs that have produced, based on the direct reports from the participants and numerous studies, an enormous contribution in the lives of several hundreds of thousands of people; created non-profit organizations that are committed to ending death by starvation by the year 2000; that visit 150,000 people in institutions on Christmas and Chanukah; that work with youth at risk so that teenagers and young people in ghettos who may otherwise be in jail or have been killed by the age of 18 are now leading productive lives.' I said, 'Without including that part, his statement about this being a fair and balanced piece was simply untrue.'

"No response. It was clear he had no interest in doing an unbiased piece. I told him everything we knew about the motives of the people he was relying upon, particularly Gutfreund. This information didn't faze him. The guy's whole attitude was 'I'll go through the motions of putting together an honest piece, but don't count on it.' I came away from that hour and a half with the feeling that I should have instead donated my time to the Red Cross. It certainly would have made more of a difference."[14]

Gelber's co-producer, Doug Hamilton, also seemed to have some objectivity problems. John Catalina, who had worked very closely with Erhard for years, said that Hamilton badgered him for several days, calling his home as late as 1 a.m., trying to get him to do an interview for the program. Catalina said that Hamilton told him it was important that Erhard be "exposed," and that those people who had been wronged be "vindicated." Hamilton also told Catalina that *60 Minutes* believed that Erhard had done a number of "very bad things to people." Hamilton exposed that *60 Minutes* had bought into the web when he said that they were "representing people who thought Erhard lived differently than he talked."[15]

Hamilton made no comment to Catalina about *60 Minutes* having any interest in finding out the truth, nor did he make any reference to any interest in the full story. By this time, the producers had given up any pretense of objectivity. Because Doug Hamilton only spoke with a small group of disaffected ex-employees, he may have thought all of Erhard's ex-employees were like the group he had spoken to. While it was true that Catalina had left Erhard's employ months earlier and had gone his own way, it was not true that Catalina shared the view that Erhard lived differently than he talked.

John Catalina had known Erhard intimately over a period of many years. Catalina had worked in various capacities for Erhard's company and for the last seven years had worked directly with Erhard. They worked together night and day. Catalina managed the boat where Erhard lived and traveled with Erhard as an aide. Catalina knew Erhard's personal and family life well.

Despite Catalina's insistence that he knew of no wrongdoing by Erhard, Hamilton suggested to Catalina over and over that he confirm the rumors Hamilton had heard from others that Erhard was into drugs, had beaten up co-workers, and made people take "secret oaths." "I told Hamilton that what he had told me about Werner was not in any way consistent with what I knew about Werner and that I considered that he and *60 Minutes* were totally wrong in what they were attempting," Catalina said. "I tried to tell Hamilton of my own observations regarding Werner. Hamilton was not interested since my observations were inconsistent with what he wanted to hear."[16]

It became more and more apparent that *60 Minutes* was not reporting. Rather it was being used to carry out a mission L. Ron Hubbard had left to his followers in the Church of Scientology: the mission to destroy Werner Erhard. As a result, Erhard's attorneys were in constant communication with the attorneys at CBS, attempting to caution them that the direction their producers were taking the show was based on false information. They warned CBS attorneys that the material they were getting was only coming from a non-representative, small faction of individuals who were clearly biased and motivated by vendettas against Erhard.[17]

One affidavit after another contradicting the

allegations was submitted by former employees,
family members, and others who had direct knowledge of the events on which the allegations against
Erhard were based. *60 Minutes* was already in possession of solid evidence that the allegations they
were to air were false. They aired the allegations anyway, without specifically acknowledging the existence of contradictory evidence.

Most of the affidavits were from people who no
longer worked for Erhard. Many of them had not
been in contact with him for years. These people
were therefore unlikely to be influenced in any way
by Erhard or by a bias towards him. But *60 Minutes*
chose to dismiss the validity of their sworn affidavits
and all the other evidence which they had in their
possession that contradicted the allegations they
would air. The only mention of this overwhelming
amount of evidence was a dismissal of it in the
announcer's final comment: "Erhard's lawyers sent
us affidavits from his sister and brother and from a
few of his close associates disputing some of the stories we heard from his children. . . ."[18]

60 Minutes never contacted one of the people
who signed these sworn affidavits either for verifi-
cation or for clarification of their statements. In fact
they never even contacted these people at all. For
example, *60 Minutes* had no fewer than six affidavits
in their possession that completely contradicted the
description of one horrifying incident depicting
Erhard as an abusive husband [described by two of
the children on the *60 Minutes* show.][19] They chose
to disregard this sworn testimony.

60 Minutes dismissed the affidavits by saying they
all came from close associates or immediate members of his family. But, for example, one of the
individuals whom *60 Minutes* dismissed by calling
a "close associate" was a business owner who hadn't

worked for Erhard for 13 years.

Locke McCorkle, before leaving Erhard's employ in 1978, worked for him as the manager of a facility which served as Erhard's office and sometimes residence. McCorkle was present at both occasions about which two of the children made allegations regarding the treatment of Erhard's ex-wife. These allegations were first made in several San Francisco Bay Area publications, and later, merely repeated by the children on *60 Minutes*.

McCorkle testified, "I have read both the articles in the *San Jose Mercury News* and *The Marin Independent Journal* which describe a dinner and meeting at the Franklin House and at which I was present. The events and circumstances described in these articles are simply not accurate. The description is stated as fact by two of Mr. Erhard's daughters who were adolescents at the time. Their recollection and characterization of the events, particularly relating to a purported attack on Mrs. Erhard, are confused at best and in many cases completely wrong."[20]

Gelber was in possession of McCorkle's affidavit months before his *60 Minutes* show was aired. He also had many other affidavits that directly refuted the children's recollections of the time when Ellen Erhard was supposedly choked until she was near death. Instead of including a statement from any one of the sworn affidavits in his possession, he chose instead to include as his star witness the very person who admitted he was the one who choked Ellen Erhard, Robert Larzelere. Larzelere had worked for Erhard for several years. Toward the end of his tenure with Erhard, Larzelere became fascinated with the occult, regularly interacting with a medium named Jach Pursel who talked with a spirit called Lazaris. Larzelere left est for a full-time involvement with the medium when Erhard flatly refused to allow him to incorporate anything occult into any est programs.

While Larzelere admitted on *60 Minutes* that he was the one who choked Ellen Erhard in 1977, he said Erhard had directed him to do it. All other accounts, including those in the sworn affidavits submitted to *60 Minutes,* say Larzelere did it on his own, totally shocking everyone present, including Erhard.

At a family dinner, Ellen Erhard surprised the family with the information that she was involved in a personal relationship with another man and had been lying to the family about that and other things. She also acknowledged that she had been gossiping about and undermining her husband. The next time the family got together again, Larzelere was present. Ellen was letting the family know how she had resolved these conflicts for herself. At one point, when she evaded a question from one of the older children, Larzelere, without prompting from anyone, suddenly walked over to her and choked her. Before Erhard or anyone could stop Larzelere, he just as quickly let go of her and sat back down.[21]

Larzelere was normally seen to be a well-balanced person. However, when some people who had known him heard that he had been taped for possible use on the *60 Minutes* show, they came forward and reported that he had actually exhibited this bizarre behavior before. A number of people said in sworn affadavits which were provided to *60 Minutes* that they had witnessed Larzalere once choke a person because that person wasn't understanding what Larzelere was saying[22] and another time he had someone hung out a fifth-floor window by his feet because the person had the "wrong attitude."[23] Julia Dederer, who worked directly with Larzelere from 1973 to 1981, declared that she had observed him exhibit strange behavior on a few occasions, especially during the last year of Larzelere's employment with est.

Dederer stated in her sworn affidavit that was submitted to *60 Minutes* that Larzelere's behavior became increasingly bizarre after he started his relationship with Lazaris in 1980.[24] According to literature provided by Concept: Synergy in Palm Beach, Florida, Lazaris is a "nonphysical entity . . . a consciousness without form— a Spark of Light, a Spark of Love—an energy that has never chosen to take human form. . . . The way Lazaris communicates to us is called channeling." The material goes on to describe how Lazaris channels only through Jach Pursel, an executive of an art gallery and publishing company in Florida, who reportedly is not aware of what is being said during the trance. Pursel has been channeling for Lazaris since October 3, 1974, and conducts regular seminars in San Francisco, Los Angeles, Seattle, Atlanta, Chicago, Palm Beach, Washington, D.C., and Fort Lee, New Jersey, where Lazaris speaks through Pursel on an "array of topics, giving both understanding of how to deal with aspects of personal growth and techniques to move forward into ever-increasing levels of self-love and personal power."[25]

Larzelere told *60 Minutes,* apparently in an attempt to justify his bizarre behavior, that he choked Ellen Erhard in order to win Erhard's approval. "Now, I can be a real soldier for him. Now, I can make him proud of me. Now, I can get him to smile at me. Now, I won't have to be afraid of him anymore," Larzelere said in the tape *60 Minutes* aired.[26]

In her statement, Dederer said she had never seen any evidence that Larzelere felt that way. "We had a close working relationship, one in which we worked directly together and confided regularly to each other our most personal feelings and thoughts on matters of work and our personal lives. . . . Never once in the years I worked with Larzelere did I ever hear him say that he was afraid of Erhard, that he acted in a way to get Erhard's approval, or that Erhard had power over him," Dederer said.[27]

She concluded her statement by saying that she thought *60 Minutes* was making a mistake if they were thinking about using Larzelere on the program. But, for *60 Minutes,* Larzelere was the perfect choice to put on the show, even though what Larzelere said was contradicted by every single affidavit submitted by the adults present at the event. The producers did not even mention the existence of the evidence related to this specific incident, much less include an interview with any one of the many people they knew about, who countered Larzelere's claim.

One of the most glaring omissions on the part of *60 Minutes* was an affidavit from one of Erhard's other daughters. Lynn Erhard, Celeste and Adair Erhard's half sister, in her sworn affidavit unequivocally refuted allegations made by her half sisters regarding a specific incident that was being reported to *60 Minutes* and which later aired on the show. Although the rest of her statement didn't respond to the alleged sexual abuse, because at the time, she had no idea her sister would make that allegation, she demonstrated the family's support for her father and made it clear that most members of the family were not in agreement with the allegations which were being made by Erhard's other daughters. While *60 Minutes* made much of the fact that it was Erhard's own daughter making the allegations, there was no attempt whatsoever by anyone from *60 Minutes* to interview his other daughter Lynn or even to check out her statement. The producers aired only the three daughters who attacked their father and concealed that they had statements from another daughter contradicting the attack and supporting her father.

While preparing his show on Erhard, it appears that Gelber may have even received conflicting stories from the people he did select for interviews. In one instance, although John Hubner said Celeste Erhard had earlier corroborated the story Dawn Damas told Hubner, Celeste says she told Gelber several times during her interview for *60 Minutes* that her father had never beaten or even hit her brother (an allegation voiced on the program).[28] Gelber could have at least reported on the inconsistencies that were revealed to him, but instead, chose to present only Ellen Erhard's friend Damas and her daughter Adair saying that the incident did happen.

Celeste said that she was there during the entire time referred to by Damas. "My father never touched my brother. In fact, during my entire childhood my father never struck or physically abused us, or allowed anyone else to do so. Neither my brother or sister ever told me to the contrary during our growing up."

In the sections of tapes that *60 Minutes* actually aired of Celeste on March 3, she appeared emotionally distraught. However, Celeste said that during most of the approximately two hours of her interview, she was not crying and was very calm. She only got upset when Gelber kept stopping the camera when he didn't like the way she answered a question and got her to rephrase it, constantly reminding her how horrible it must have been. "He got me real frustrated," she said. "I had watched them tape Adair and they didn't do that to her. She had all the right answers I guess."

In fact, Celeste said that Adair was only parroting her when they were interviewed for the show because Adair had been unable to remember any of the events that they were being asked about. By that time, Celeste had just enrolled in a drug rehabilitation program, but said that Adair was still heavy into drugs. Celeste said that on their way to be filmed for *60 Minutes,* Adair was smoking a joint in the car and was stoned by the time they got to the interview.

After the *60 Minutes* interviews were completed, Celeste said that Gelber introduced her and Adair to an independent movie producer who acquired a contract for them with Lorimar pictures. Celeste said that John Hubner was going to write the screenplay for the Lorimar movie. Celeste, who by now was totally disgusted with herself and the role she was playing in destroying her father, refused to sign the contract despite repeated intense pressure from her mother, siblings, Damas, and Hubner. Celeste said that one time her mother actually put a pen in her hand and told her to sign the contract. She never did, and Lorimar eventually shelved the movie.[29]

When I asked Erhard about his children's accusations, he responded, ''Of course I am deeply saddened by my children saying these horrible things about me and I regret the impact on my friends, associates, and the other people who have supported me. The recent media coverage could make their magnanimity look foolish. While some of the people with whom I've discussed this have found it hard to believe, what I am most concerned about in all this is my children's and my family's well being. While I cannot escape the conclusion that the environment I provided for my children while they were growing up was flawed, it is clear to me that something or someone has intervened in my children's attitude, character, interpretation of the past and even their memory of the facts."[30]

Erhard said the allegations made against him by a few of his former associates and three of his children were all "just plain false". He said, "That fact is less important to me than what has to have been done to my children for them to make these allegations. It can't be explained with the idea that my children had no other way to deal with their differences with me. The accusations aired by the press supposedly all happened years ago and as anyone who has any true knowledge of my relationship with my children knows, I've always made myself available to them whenever they've had anything to say. I listened openly if they were pointing out a mistake I made. I acknowledged it and endeavored not to repeat it. When I disagreed with what they said, I didn't make what they said wrong, but rather told them that I had a different point of view or a different memory of the facts."

He said his relationship with Celeste and Adair had been fine until just before they were interviewed by *60 Minutes.* After that, they cut off all contact with him. Erhard remembers that in the weeks just before someone got Adair together with *60 Minutes,* that the two of them had lunch together with a friend, and that on a separate occasion, he and Adair and Adair's boyfriend had just been to a dinner party Erhard gave in support of a local performing arts endeavor. Erhard said, "Although she said she had to do it quietly, Adair and I had been meeting together and speaking over the phone. We were working closely together to deal with the unresolved emotions she was experiencing over her recent separation from her husband. Adair and I had generally gotten along well in the past except for one time when she got very upset because she felt that I had insulted her at a debutante event she was attending.

While, from time to time we had differences, we always resolved those differences and she and I were close.''

"Adair and I respected each other. She even asked her school, Emma Willard Academy, to invite me to be the speaker at her graduation exercises. I was pleased about what that said about our relationship because some kids want to keep their parents hidden from their friends. I was actually shocked by her attack on me, it was so inconsistent with the love and regard we shared for each other.''

He said the situation with Celeste was similar. He had been supporting her in her battle to regain herself. "But the last time I saw Celeste before she appeared on *60 Minutes,* from out of nowhere she suddenly began to accuse me of having done all manner of bad things to my children in the past. While Celeste knew full well that I never struck any of my children, she said on that occasion that she remembered me being physically violent with her brother St. John. I couldn't believe what I was hearing because I never struck my children and they knew I never would, but I tried to be gentle with her given what I knew she was dealing with in life. I said 'look, Celeste, I don't know where you got the things you're saying, and I don't know why you're suddenly saying them now, but if you'll look into your own memory without anyone else's suggestions, I think you'll realize they're just not true.' There were times over the past few years when Celeste was just not herself, and I assumed that this occasion was one of them.''

Erhard said he reminded Celeste about when St. John was a schoolboy, listening to and memorizing tapes of the comedian, Richard Pryor. "St. John would get his flashlight and make a tent out of his covers and listen to Pryor's tapes at night when he was supposed to be asleep," Erhard said. "While he got reprimanded when he used some of Pryor's material in front of us, he could use other parts of it very skillfully at the right time. I told Celeste that I thought that she was actually present on the afternoon I was the angriest I ever got with St. John. He had been repeatedly getting poor grades, even though he was intelligent and had the extra support of tutoring. He had admitted that the poor grades came from just not doing his schoolwork, not applying himself. He had promised on more than one occasion to get off his duff and get into his schoolwork. He just hadn't kept his promise and I was at the end of my rope with him and really reaming him out. At the end of a particularly harsh sentence, St. John blurted out a timely Pryorism. He said 'I know, you brought me into this world and you can take me out.' I couldn't help but burst out laughing. St. John's joke settled me down and I began to have a real discussion with him. When I reminded Celeste of that very humorous incident, I thought I noticed a sign of recognition in her face, but she said nothing and left."

Erhard said the next time he heard from Celeste was a few weeks later when he read what she said about him in John Hubner's articles. "I think it would be legitimate to say that the press used my children," Erhard said, "and that the way they were used got them completely stuck with what they had said. For them to recant would be so embarrassing that they would have to stick with their story no matter what. But, to both stick with the story and at the same time be able to live with themselves, they would have to avoid being reminded of the truth. They would have to put up a wall to keep out the people they knew, who knew the truth about the allegations they made against me."

He said that as a matter of fact, a woman who had worked closely with him for many years and knew Adair and his relationship with her very well told him she had almost bumped into Adair at a restaurant right after the *60 Minutes* program. Erhard said, "She told me, 'while I was in the lobby waiting for a table Adair walked in. But, as I started to say hello to Adair, she looked up and recognized me, and when she did she turned around and fled out of the restaurant.'

"I am left with enormous admiration for my daughter Celeste, who has had the courage to correct what she said about me and to tell the truth," Erhard said. "It is a miracle given the way Celeste was used that our relationship is restored. Celeste showed extraordinary strength of character in coming to visit me. What Celeste and her husband said had been done to manipulate her by those who waste their lives hating me, and by a few unscrupulous members of the media looking to advance their careers, was a story of so great a violence to the human spirit, that it was hard to believe. I am proud of Celeste that she had the integrity to regain herself and is able to hold her head up high."

Erhard said at first he thought Celeste might be making up what she had been through to justify what she had done to him. "But she had hard evidence of the inducement, the pressure and the brainwashing as she called it, that she'd been through. As I listened to her in detail I could see that the 'hard to believe' was true. Also what she recounted explained much that I had not understood about my children's behavior with me in the past.

"While it has become clear to me that forces have worked to undermine my relationship with my children and turn them against me, ultimately, it is I who am responsible for my children. Actually I accept the responsibility gladly because if I am not willing to be responsible for what is wrong, I disempower myself in setting it right. It's not a matter of blaming myself, or making myself guilty about it. That's a cheap way out. It's rather a matter of looking at the situation and seeing that I am responsible, and therefore can clean it up. And that is what I am committed to doing. My children are wonderful people, and they always loved honesty and forthrightness. Recovering that foundation I should be able, with their cooperation, to sort out this mess and leave my family whole.''

Erhard related a story about Adair at the age of 12 or 13 shoplifting and getting caught by her mother who told Erhard. ''I sat down with Adair and we had a long talk about honesty and integrity. We discussed what the absence of that insidiously did to the quality of a person's life, and what the presence of that did to empower a person. She and I agreed that she would take the things she still had back to the store and offer to work over the Christmas holiday to pay the store back for what she had already used. Adair really brightened up at the opportunity to restore her integrity and demonstrate to herself that underneath it all she was a person who loved the truth. As I said, my children are really great people.''

Erhard concluded by saying, ''I too have a great respect for the truth. However, I must use my energy to make my family whole and trust that somehow time will reveal whatever the truth is behind this attack on me.''[31]

One cannot help but wonder what happened to *60 Minutes'* concern for the truth. They knew about and had access to the people who had contrary evidence for most, if not all of the allegations made against Erhard. They had the enormous resources of CBS to check with these people. They had reason to strongly suspect the bias and malice of the people making the accusations. David Gelber and Doug Hamilton could not avoid being aware that they were in the midst of an actual campaign to ruin Erhard.

Gelber and Hamilton seemed to have lost their sense of perspective, fairness and critical judgment by buying into the conspiracy against Erhard, the person who Gelber had started out calling "a fascinating man." While the *60 Minutes* segment on Erhard was skillfully crafted and cleverly presented, with one very significant exception, it had nothing new. The producers allowed the direction of their piece on Erhard to be handed to them. They accepted as research what had already been put together by Hubner and a few members of the San Francisco press.

The *60 Minutes* show would have been nothing more than a mere rehash of the defamatory statements that had already been published and republished by the local press had it not been for coming up with one new sensational allegation. While Erhard's reputation had been battered, given the powerful evidence contradicting the truth of all the old allegations, his life was still viable. However, *60 Minutes* came up with a new and completely monstrous allegation that turned out to be what the conspiracy had been looking for. The final solution for eliminating Erhard was provided by Erhard's daughter Deborah Pimental, his youngest child from his first marriage.

In this ultimate accusation, which she would deliver, Scientology would fulfill the edict of its founder to destroy the enemy. The Afremow group would make good on another threat Randy Loftin voiced,

"You tell Erhard I'll get him."[32] Paul Gutfreund would fulfill the ambition for which he stopped working and spent his full time for nearly three years. Ellen Erhard would fulfill her vendetta of hatred expressed in a concise sentence she is reported to have said to Dawn Damas, "It's time to get this motherfucker."[33] *60 Minutes* would fulfill the producer's pledge to "represent the people who thought Erhard lived differently than he talked".

On national television, before an audience of millions, Pimental said that 11 years earlier Erhard had raped her sister and added that 15 years earlier he had molested her (Pimental). That allegation was the bullet used to fell Erhard. Against the background of 20 years of planted media stories about Werner Erhard, Pimental's new charges needed no proof to do their job, they needed only to be uttered on the air. That fact could not have escaped the people who got together to try to convince the world, that Erhard was not the man he seemed to be.

When Pimental was first contacted for an interview, it was by John Hubner, the reporter from the *San Jose Mercury News.* At that time, she refused to talk to him. It was later reported by another family member, in whom Pimental had confided, that Pimental said that Hubner tried to induce her to be interviewed using the fact that she had just given birth to her first child. She said he pointed out that with that added responsibility, she could probably use the money she could make by helping him to write a book and that the publicity of being interviewed would make that possible. Pimental said that Hubner told her that she owed it to her new baby to take advantage of this opportunity.[34]

Dawn Damas, Ellen Erhard's close friend; Landon Carter, who had provided one of the affidavits which the judge sealed in the Afremow case; Celeste Erhard, the daughter who later recanted the allegations against her father; and Robert Larzelere, the man who had choked Ellen Erhard all worked on Pimental or her sister to persuade them to join the conspiracy against their father.

It took work to entice Pimental to participate in the plot to destroy Erhard but the work paid off. Hubner offered her money. Bob Larzelere provided encouragement. Gail Brashear was attending a seminar at the Cathedral Hill Hotel shortly after the *60 Minutes* piece when she overheard Bob Larzelere in the phone booth next to her. He was in the hotel for a session with the medium for Lazaris. Brashear stepped forward, though fearful of retribution, and submitted the following comments by Larzelere. Her sworn statement quotes Larzelere as saying, "What a good job we did, I'm complete now. We got Debbie to testify."[35]

The sister Pimental said was raped [her name is not used throughout this book to protect her privacy] refused to publicly confirm or deny the accusations. Even though members of the conspiracy contacted her, she never would speak to a reporter. She also refused to respond to Erhard's pleas to talk with him.

Pimental never discussed the possibility of going on *60 Minutes* with any member of her family. However, after her interview was taped and before the show was aired, she told her mother, Pat Fry, Erhard's first wife, what she had done.[36]

Fry, deeply disturbed by her daughter's actions, warned Erhard of what he would see on *60 Minutes.* But, Erhard was defenseless against such an accusation, other than to publicly call his daughter a liar, something he was unwilling to do. What does one do to prove a negative, how does one prove that something didn't happen? Erhard's attorneys thought that the accusation was so serious, so certain of irreparably destroying his reputation forever, that if he provided any evidence at all to *60 Minutes* that the accusation was false, they would at least refrain from broadcasting Pimental's claim, until they fully investigated. Erhard hoped that in that full investigation he could somehow show enough evidence that the accusation was false, that *60 Minutes* would, in fairness, finally not broadcast the allegation.

While Erhard knew that a lie detector test was not by itself conclusive evidence, he knew of no other way to prove that something someone said had happened, had in fact not happened. He felt certain that passing a lie detector test would be sufficient to cause *60 Minutes* to at least question the validity of the accusation. *60 Minutes* knew that once they made the accusation public, the damage caused to Erhard's life by just having someone make the accusation could never be repaired, even if later it was proven false. He had no choice but to trust his life to *60 Minutes*' sense of professionalism and fair play.

A polygraph test, which Erhard took, was administered and evaluated by Victor C. Kaufman, recognized as one of the leading polygraph experts in the world. The test was administered under the auspices of the New York Lie Detection Laboratories, New York's leading polygraph laboratory with a national reputation.

Kaufman's written report indicated that there was a range of scores in which a test would be inconclusive. However, on the other hand, he went on to state that a score of plus 6 or higher by an examinee is a reliable criterion for truthfulness, while a score of minus 6 or lower is reliable evidence that the answer given was a lie. The rating for the examinee, Werner Erhard, was a plus 10. The relevant questions that Erhard submitted to on the test were "Have you ever sexually molested any of your children? Have you ever raped any of your children? Have you ever sexually abused any of your children?" He answered no to all of these questions. In the section of the report that dealt with the conclusions of the examinee's test, given the way Erhard scored in his test, Kaufman unequivocally stated that there was no deception in Erhard's responses and that he had answered all the questions truthfully.[37]

When Erhard showed the report of his polygraph test to his attorneys, they were sure *60 Minutes* would take notice this time, and submitted copies of the full report to CBS. They also sent a letter which offered for Erhard to take another test under CBS's supervision with any expert of their choice. Erhard's attorneys requested that CBS not air any allegations on which the second test confirmed the results of the test Erhard had already taken.[38]

But to the amazement of Erhard's attorneys, *60 Minutes* ignored the evidence and declined the offer.[39] They did not even pretend to pause for a moment in putting together the segment which would, in just 18 minutes, destroy Erhard's reputation built on 20 years of contribution to the lives of hundreds of thousands of people, not to mention his contribution to the very survival of people in many Third World countries. Apparently, the producers' arrogance prevented them from even questioning what they were doing, let alone making any attempt at investigating the extraordinarily convincing evidence supplied to them by Erhard's attorneys.

Those seeking Erhard's destruction have tried many times to use the nation's courtrooms to achieve their aim, but he has never lost a single case brought against him. At the prompting of his detractors, he has been thoroughly investigated by government agencies, but these investigations have only served to confirm Erhard's clear record.

Werner Erhard's brother, Harry Rosenberg, said, "When all this failed, the web constituted the *60 Minutes* show as a kind of kangaroo courtroom in which to try Werner. The self appointed prosecutor, judge and jury in this courtroom would be *60 Minutes* and the others connected in the web against him. They would also be the only witnesses. In this trial, there would be no evidence, no proof offered, there would only be accusations. There would not be one shred of material evidence. Instead, at this grotesque trial, the accusations would be woven together into a dramatic story, and one accusation would be built upon the other in order to make the prosecution's case. Not one of the witnesses with testimony contradicting the accusations would be allowed in the courtroom. This was a trial where the accused was presumed guilty without any proof, and where the judge decided to deny the accused any right to defend himself. To this day there remains not one piece of hard evidence for any of the allegations ever made against Werner."

60 Minutes made sure that the public was not allowed a seat on the jury. They did not make available to the public any of the contradictory evidence they possessed, depriving the public of the opportunity to make up its own mind. For example, in contrast to the full play given to the horrendous final allegation, there was not even a mention that Erhard, taking the only avenue available to him to prove his innocence, had submitted himself to a lie detector test administered by a recognized expert.[40] *60*

Minutes acted to conceal from the public any knowledge that Erhard had taken and passed that test conclusively, and that the results of the test diametrically contradicted the accusations of the prosecution's star witness. *60 Minutes* only announced its verdict to the public. Erhard was found guilty in a courtroom from which there is no appeal. In effect his accusers appointed themselves not only the judge, prosecution, jury, and only witnesses, but his executioners as well.

Erhard's professional public relations advisors, including the highly respected John Scanlon, strongly advised against Erhard's appearance on *60 Minutes*. Erhard said that they told him that *60 Minutes* had already demonstrated that nothing he could provide would make a bit of difference to produce any sense of balance in the program they intended to air. They reminded him that *60 Minutes* alone would decide whether or not to use his statement, and could show only the parts they liked and edit out what they didn't.

The advice turned out to be dead accurate. While Erhard declined to be interviewed, he did send a brief four-sentence statement asking that if read, it be read in its entirety. The statement said he was not going to respond to the allegations because to do so at this time ''would only serve to further publicly exploit my family and there has already been enough of that.'' He said that what he was going to do, was to concentrate on healing and restoring his family.

The last sentence said, ''However, I reserve the right, at some future date, to set the record straight.'' *60 Minutes* producers edited out this sentence. By doing so, they made it seem like Erhard was admitting to the allegations and was now going to make it up to his family.

Erhard said, "I have no quarrel with the press when they do their job with integrity. In this case they did not. In any case, I wish they would leave my family alone and stop exploiting my children."

Perhaps the last word on *60 Minutes'* treatment of Erhard should come from a respected member of the media itself. Carl Bernstein, author and co-winner of the 1973 Pulitzer Prize for his investigative coverage of the Watergate burglary for the *Washington Post,* writing recently about the need for unbiased and honest scrutiny of public figures by the media, wrote, "In actually covering existing American life, the media—weekly, daily, hourly—break new ground in getting it wrong. The coverage is distorted by celebrity and the worship of celebrity; by the reduction of news to gossip, which is the lowest form of news; by sensationalism, which is always a turning away from a society's real condition; and by a political and social discourse that we—the press—are turning into a sewer."[41]

[1] Transcript and videotape of *60 Minutes*, March 3, 1991
[2] Interview with Anthony Pellicano, July 5, 1992.
[3] Welkos, *Los Angeles Times,* December 29, 1991.
[4] Interview with Celeste Erhard, February 22, 1992.
[5] Sworn affidavit by Ted Heisig, October 29, 1991.
[6] *Village Voice,* January, 1991.
[7] Welkos, *Los Angeles Times,* December 29, 1991.
[8] Letter to William Barnes from David Gelber, November 9, 1990.
[9] Herb Caen, *San Francisco Chronicle,* November 1990
[10] Letter to William Barnes from David Gelber, November 9, 1990.
[11] Interview with Celeste Erhard, February 22, 1992; Interview with Pat Fry, February 22, 1992.
[12] Werner Erhard v. CBS et al, March 3, 1992.
[13] Interview with Celeste Erhard, February 22, 1992; Interview with Christian Santangelo, February 23, 1992.
[14] Interview with Art Schreiber, January 4, 1992.
[15] Interview with John Catalina, July 3, 1992; sworn affadavit by John Catalina, December 22, 1990.
[16] Interview with John Catalina, July 3, 1992; sworn affadavit by John Catalina, December 22, 1990.

[17] Correspondence from Martin Leaf to CBS' Doug Jacobs, November 30, 1990; correspondence from Charles O. Morgan Jr. to Douglas Jacobs, December 14, 1990; correspondence from Charles O. Morgan Jr. to Jonathan Sternberg, January 21, 1991, January 29, 1991, February 12, 1991, February 23, 1991, and February 25, 1991.

[18] Transcript and videotape of *60 Minutes*, March 3, 1991.

[19] Statement by Locke McCorkle, January 18, 1991; Statement by Jack Rafferty, January 18, 1991; Statement by Lynn Erhard, undated; Statement by Joan Rosenberg, February 25, 1991; Statement by Harry Rosenberg, February 20, 1991; Statement by Gonneke Spits February 25, 1991.

[20] Statement by Locke McCorkle, January 18, 1991.

[21] Statement by Harry Rosenberg, February 20, 1991.

[22] Statement by David Norris, February 25, 1991.

[23] Statement by Bill Palmer, November 27, 1991.

[24] Interview with Julia Dederer, June 22, 1992; affidavit by Julie Dederer, February 26, 1991.

[25] *The Lazaris Material,* Concept: Synergy, Inside cover, p. 31.

[26] Transcript and videotape of *60 Minutes*, March 3, 1991.

[27] Statement of Julia Dederer, February 26, 1991.

[28] Interview with Celeste Erhard, February 22, 1992.

[29] Telephone conversation with Julie Waxman of Lorimar pictures, May 5, 1992.

[30] Interview with Werner Erhard, September 15, 1991.

[31] Interview with Werner Erhard, September 15, 1991.

[32] Statement by Clay Waltman, May 4, 1992, regarding serving summons to Randy Loftin on April 27, 1992.

[33] Statement by Dave Rios, February 21, 1992.

[34] Affidavit by Harry Rosenberg, undated.

[35] Affidavit by Gail Brashear, January 26, 1992.

[36] Interview with Pat Fry, February 22, 1992.

[37] Report by Victor C. Kaufman, New York Lie Detection Laboratories, September 4, 1990.

[38] Correspondence from Charles O. Morgan Jr. to Jonathan Sternberg of CBS, February 12, 1991.

[39] Correspondence from Jonathan Sternberg to Charles O. Morgan Jr., February 14, 1991.

[40] Transcript and videotape of *60 Minutes*, March 3, 1991

[41] Carl Bernstein, "The Idiot Culture, *The New Republic,* June 8, 1992, p. 22.

CHAPTER VI
A FAMILY ASUNDER

Over his 20-year career, Erhard had survived periodic malignings in the media. More and more people kept participating in his programs, and the number and quality of people who supported his work just kept growing. Without the ultimate accusations made by Erhard's daughter, Deborah Pimental, even *60 Minutes*' raking over of the old allegations might have been dismissed by the viewer as an undeserved attack on Erhard by a few disgruntled former associates and two daughters sniping at their father.

Without the drama and what was said merely for effect, Pimental made exactly five statements. These five statements taken together destroyed her father's reputation forever.

Number one, she said that she had never spoken publicly about her father before. Number two, she said she had never told anyone, until *60 Minutes,* that her father had sexually abused her. Number three, she claimed that when she was 16 years old her father molested her. Number four, she stated that Erhard admitted having intercourse with her sister. Number five, she said that in fact, her father had raped her sister.

When the interviewer on *60 Minutes* said "she's never spoken publicly about her father before," it was implicit in the statement that there was some old deep-seated issue Pimental had with her father. If there was such an issue, it could explain the unusual fact that no one had heard these accusations from Pimental before. While this statement was designed to make what Pimental would say more believable, the statement that she had not spoken publicly about her father before is patently false.

For example, during her freshman year at Mills College, she granted an interview to the daughter of Walter Cronkite. Kathy Cronkite was writing about what it was like to be the child of a celebrity, and comparing other children's experiences with her own. In that interview Pimental talked about the close relationship she and her siblings had with their father, and how much she loved and appreciated him. In fact, Pimental ended that interview saying she'd like to let people know that "you can actually have a relationship that isn't full of terrible things. I just want people to know that all they need to do is be honest and say all those things that they don't want to say. . . . I just want to say I love my father a lot. As much as you can, I guess."[1] Pimental used these words to report on her relationship with her father less than two years after the time she was now claiming to a national audience that he had molested her.

Even earlier, at age 17, Pimental dedicated her senior picture in the high school yearbook to her father. The last verse of her poem of dedication reads: "He comes into my life; he shares his wisdom. I am no longer blind; I look and see the way. . . . ''[2] Telling the truth about the many public statements she had made about her father, especially when some of those statements were made not very long after the time she was claiming he molested her, would make the claim hard to believe.

Pimental added to the lie that she had never publicly spoken about her father, by telling a second lie in the next of her five statements. She said she had never told anyone about being molested until that moment. In an article that appeared hours before the *60 Minutes* broadcast, John Hubner wrote in the *San Jose Mercury News* that Pimental, who had recently turned 31, said that she had kept the alleged molestation by her father secret all these years and was now only admitting it to "let my sister know she wasn't alone.''[3]

Not true, says Pimental's mother, Pat Fry. Fry stated that shortly after the 1976 incident Pimental was now calling a molestation, her daughter told her all about it.[4]

Pimental told the *60 Minutes* interviewer, "I don't have a problem saying that it happened. I don't like describing it. But I don't have a problem admitting that he molested me.''[5] What Pimental didn't mind calling a molestation but said did not want to describe, she had already described to her mother shortly after the incident.

Her mother said that in a conversation between the two of them, her daughter was telling her about a trip she had recently been on with her father. She fell asleep on the bed while in his room reading a magazine. Later, when Erhard had also drifted off while reading, he rolled over in his sleep, his hand fell across Pimental's breast and startled her. She was

16 at the time. She told her mother nothing else happened and that she hadn't mentioned it to her father.
Pimental said she was okay about it and didn't think
it meant anything. Of course, her mother took pains
in the discussion with Pimental to satisfy herself that
what happened was innocent, an accident, and that
her daughter was not upset or concerned by what
did happen. Neither of them ever felt the need to
say anything to Erhard. Fry was satisfied by what
her daughter told her and forgot the whole thing.[6]

The next time Fry heard anything about this incident was 15 years later, between the time that *60
Minutes* taped Pimental's interview and the time the
show aired on March 3, 1991. Fry had been visiting
her daughter at her home in Hawaii. Pimental told
her mother that she had gone to San Francisco to
be interviewed by *60 Minutes,* and that the broadcast would air her claim that she was molested. Fry
couldn't believe it. She said they actually had an
argument about it. "Well, I shouldn't say an argument, but our voices were raised," said Fry. "I was
really shocked that my daughter would actually go
on *60 Minutes* and say that."[7]

After two lies to set it up, Pimental's third statement, that her father had molested her, was at the
very least an intentional deception. But it all helped
to make what came next believable.

She next told *60 Minutes* that her father raped her
sister. But even with the three fabrications to set it
up, this was so outrageous, so horrendous an accusation, that it needed further bolstering. Pimental
made this ultimate accusation believable by telling
60 Minutes interviewer Ed Bradley her fourth lie.
She said, "What he did say when I confronted him
about it was that there had been sexual intercourse
and that had been a nurturing experience for my
sister."[8]

In a signed affidavit made after she saw the *60 Minutes* show, Lynn Erhard, Pimental's other sister states, "My father did not say anything like that. He, in fact, said the opposite. He said he did not have intercourse with my sister."[9] When I interviewed Erhard in Mexico, he also told me that he never said any such thing. Months later when I talked at length to Pimental's mother, Pat Fry, she too confirmed that Erhard had said no such thing.

Fry talked about a meeting she and Erhard set up to bring the family together to address the accusation made by Pimental's sister. Erhard said that he first heard about the rape accusation in early 1987 when his daughter, Pimental's sister, called him on the telephone. "She called me and said '[her brother] came up with this idea that you raped me.' And I said 'What? Well you have to tell him the truth!' I thought that was weird, strange. I couldn't figure it out. How would my son come up with the idea that I had raped his sister? But it turned out that he didn't come up with the idea. His sister told him just that."[10]

Pimental's representation on *60 Minutes* that she confronted Erhard is contradicted by the facts. What actually happened was that Erhard paid for his daughter Pimental and his son to fly to San Francisco to meet with the other children, their mother and himself. Fry said that while there was some hemming and hawing, she was adamant that the meeting happen. Fry insisted that everyone get together and stay together until everything was settled.[11] The people I spoke to who were present at the meeting said that Erhard made himself fully available to resolve the accusation which he had said from the very beginning was not true. Fry corroborated Lynn Erhard's sworn statement about what her father said at that meeting. Fry stated categorically that Erhard told the family that he did not have intercourse with his daughter.

By withholding the fact that she had publicly praised her father and professed her love for him; by characterizing an innocent brush of her father's hand as a molestation; by fabricating the story that she, trying to appear like other molested children, had kept that secret for years; and by telling the lie that her father had admitted incest with her sister, Pimental had effectively set up the *60 Minutes* audience to believe her fifth and final statement. While her sister had refused to ever speak to a reporter herself, Pimental said that her sister told her that her father had raped her.

Although Fry does not believe that the accusations that Pimental made against her father in the press are true, she has had a hard time being in the middle. She is very close to her children and hates it that some of them have such an awful relationship with their father. She was hesitant to talk about the situation, but being a woman of enormous integrity, was not able to sit back and watch her ex-husband be so viciously defamed.

It is clear that Erhard was not traditional, not a conventional father. On the other hand, by all accounts when his children were young, they were devoted to him and he to them. Clearly they were well cared for, supported and nurtured, however the circumstances in which they grew up were unconventional. For example, their father was rarely home. He travelled extensively. Even when he was in town, he usually worked at night and slept in the house where he worked.

Erhard's daughter Lynn said it didn't occur to the children for years that it was odd that they had to make appointments to see their father. "It never even dawned on me that that was strange until years later," she said. "I didn't grow up with a father so I had no picture of the way it was supposed to be," Lynn said, speaking about her very early childhood when her father was not present at all. "I had no concept that it was strange to have to set up an appointment to see your father. I knew that he was really busy. It wasn't until much later, really until I kind of pulled away and stood on the outside and looked in."[12]

She also talked about a private meeting with her brother and sisters after her sister told them she had been raped. They all came to the conclusion about how strange their family life had been. "I think we were all kind of in that same space at the same time. And we never talked about it before that we thought it was strange. That's just the way it was. Now, I think it's strange."

Erhard didn't have much time to spend with his children. He took them on trips with him whenever he could. He made sure that the people who helped manage his schedule knew that he wanted to be in regular contact with his children, to see them as often as his schedule allowed, and to know immediately when any of his children tried to reach him so that he could get back to them right away.

Gonneke Spits, who knew the family well from having worked with Erhard, addressed the difference between what someone might call a traditional father versus Erhard. She said that one of the things all of Erhard's children had a hard time understanding was that "Werner was not the kind of person you can own. He belonged to his commitments. His attention was on making a contribution, not on being somebody's best friend, father, or husband."[13] The children's varied attempts at resolving this issue for themselves was not always successful.

Spits thinks that Erhard trusted his children to understand that and to be on his side—to not hold against him the fact that he was committed to his work and consequently not around all the time when they were young. "If he were a different person, a more regular guy, he probably could have worked it out with them," said Spits.

Erhard knows that he's now paying the price for not honoring tradition. "I never tried to gain my children's approval. In fact, I was careful as they were growing up not to do things merely to get them to like me."[14] Erhard's way of being with his children, his way of relating to them and supporting them worked for them when they were children. Their letters to him, what they said about him to other family members and in public, all indicate that they were nurtured and well supported. They had all expressed how proud they were of their father. But, some of them developed problems with their father as they struggled to become adults. As adults, when they looked back on their childhood and saw that the circumstances were unusual, they reinterpreted their experience of their life with their father and his relationship with them. For some, the problems with their father were obviously serious.

While Pimental was in college studying Spanish, Erhard arranged for her to live with a friend's family in Costa Rica for awhile. Lynn thinks that maybe her sister found out from that experience what a conventional family life was like, something Erhard's children had never experienced.[15]

"From the time I reunited with my family," Erhard said, "until years later when Deborah came back from Costa Rica, she and I had an extraordinary relationship. Both of us held up the relationship as an example of what was possible between a father and a daughter. But when she returned from

Costa Rica, she had decided that, as a father, I was not the way I should be. I never quite understood what she found wrong with the way I had been during those years when we both thought the relationship was extraordinary."[16]

Erhard said that he believes all children go through a rite of passage in their teens where they stop identifying with their parents, but that had never happened with Pimental. "Maybe she was experiencing a late need to exert her independence," he said. "But in that process, she somehow developed a resentment towards me. It seemed that she would only be satisfied if I were willing to acknowledge that who I was, was wrong, and promise to become the person she thought I ought to be."

Erhard said that Pimental went from acknowledging him as her teacher to resenting that fact. "She decided that my support of her development was somehow an attempt to use her. Deborah became more and more resentful and angry. She ultimately became so angry that she refused to communicate with most members of the family. It was as though she didn't want to hear or have to relate to anything inconsistent with her view of me."

Erhard told me that he was sorry that his daughter fabricated statements about him that were untrue. He said given the frame of mind Pimental had developed, she must have blocked out the experience of years of shared love, admiration, and respect. "I think she forgot all the letters she had written to me, all the public statements she had made, and all the times she had shared our relationship in family gatherings. I think she looked through her history for anything that she could now interpret as malice on my part, and no matter how innocent it might have been, reinvented it as proof that I was some terrible person. I think that she took the mistakes I made in raising my children, the kind of mistakes all parents make, and blew them out of proportion."

Erhard said Pimental somehow put this all together into a picture of a man that was horrible enough to have raped her sister. "She was so ready to believe the worst, that when her sister accused me of rape, I don't think Deborah even questioned the accusation. Given her frame of mind, she somehow dismissed that there was not one piece of evidence, not even circumstantial evidence, to support the allegation.

"Deborah couldn't hear anything I had to say. In fact, she heard me say things I didn't say.

"Apparently Deborah ignored the fact that everyone else, including her mother, sister and brother, all had doubts that her sister was telling the truth." Erhard said that Pimental, in addition to reinterpreting her own experience, ignored her observations of the personal relationship between her sister and her father from the time the rape supposedly happened up until the time her sister made the claim nine years later. Also, she blocked out what she knew about her sister's tendencies. The fact that Erhard had subjected himself to a lie detector test, and that the resulting score was so conclusive did not cause Pimental to question her judgement. It seems she rejected out of hand the only objective evidence that existed for proving the allegation true or false.

Erhard said he does not believe Pimental was evil. His only criticism would be that her idealism had somehow taken on a tone of self-righteousness after she returned from Costa Rica. "With all the distortions in her thinking about me, I believe she lost her ability to see reason. She lost her sense of perspective. Apparently, she felt fully justified in appoint-

ing herself my sole judge and jury, but, there was
no trial of the facts, because in her mind I was
already guilty. That there was so much evidence to
cause doubt about the validity of the accusation
made no difference in her verdict.''

Erhard also thinks that with her view of him,
Pimental couldn't tolerate the regard most family
members had for him or the relationship he enjoyed
with people, some of whom she knew and admired.
While he doesn't believe she intended to stop the
contributions he might make, Erhard thinks she just
wanted the world to judge him based on her view,
rather than on his contributions.

Apparently no one in the family agreed with
Pimental's verdict, and clearly they were against the
sentence she imposed and executed. Her brother, her
sister, and her mother, all of whom had doubts about
the validity of the allegation against Erhard, were
apparently horrified by what Pimental did to her
father. She confided in no one, except the accusing
sister, that she was going to be interviewed by *60
Minutes*. Surprisingly, even this sister had reason to
doubt the legitimacy of putting her unproven accusation in the press. Pat Fry said the accusing sister
later told her that she had cautioned Pimental and
asked her ''to think long and hard about making her
accusation public.''[17] Obviously, Pimental was absolutely convinced she was morally right. *60 Minutes*
provided the opportunity for her to carry out the
sentence she had imposed on her father.

''What does a father say about being executed by
his own daughter?'' Erhard asked. ''The first thing
you do, is look to see what you did wrong. You look
to see what you might have done to deserve execu-
tion. I've been through all that many times. I certainly made mistakes in raising my children, and
given the chance, I wouldn't make those mistakes

again. I also saw that I had been naive about the forces working to turn my children against me. But all that soul-searching never really produced a fully satisfactory explanation of my daughter's behavior," Erhard said.[18]

"Many of my friends have said that while Deborah may have been worked on by forces outside my control, and while she may have had problems of her own that left her feeling that she had the right to pass judgement on me, there must have been something wrong with me, something wrong with the kind of father I was, something wrong in my family, for four of my children to attack me. They said, 'You have to take responsibility for that and explain how it happened.'

"Am I responsible for my children's attack on me? Am I responsible for the turmoil in my family? Certainly I am responsible. But, that is a different question than 'am I to blame for it?' Obviously, if I had been a different person, it all would have turned out differently, but that does not mean that the kind of person I have been caused it all. The facts are simple. Given the forces working on my children, given the kind of people my children are, and given the person I am, this was the outcome.

"Was there something I could have done to prevent it all from turning out this way? Yes, given what I now know, given what I have found out over the last six months, I feel certain I could have provided things in my relationship with my children which would have caused it all to turn out differently. But, I did not provide those things. I certainly took good care of my children, and saw the evidence that our relationship was nurturing to them. But, I did not devote my life to my children. I devoted my life to making the greatest contribution I could. I could have put my children first, but I didn't. I trusted them to respect my decision. I trusted them to recognize and take advantage of the empowerment available to them in the work to which I devoted my life. I could have done something else, but that's what I did. Frankly, while I wish it had turned out differently with most of my children, I have no regrets regarding what I chose to do with my life.

"I am responsible for my choices and the consequences. I find no one guilty. I blame no one. I take full responsibility for the whole thing, not as a way to make myself wrong, but as a way of empowering myself to clean up this mess. At the same time, I look to empower the others involved by giving them the opportunity to be responsible as well for their own actions. In that way, we can work together to clean up the mess. For me, while none of us is innocent, neither are any of us guilty. The point is not who was bad or wrong, but given what has transpired, the point is to do what needs to be done to heal everyone and go on with life productively and with satisfaction and fulfillment."

Erhard said that of the thousands of rationalizations, justifications, and explanations he's heard over the years, not one of them ever enlivened or empowered the people who were gripped by them. As a matter of fact, he said it was only when people could let go of the explanations and justifications, that they could deal effectively with what happened, complete it, and get on with their lives.

"What Deborah did is just what Deborah did. And all of the trying to figure it out, trying to justify it, trying to explain it, didn't alter a thing. It might make somebody feel better about it, but what it amounts to is just a lot of mental gyrations. Where I came out, after all the looking, all the questioning, and all the 'maybe it was this,' and 'maybe it was that,' was that what happened is just what happened. My family is my family and I love them."

Erhard said he feels no animosity towards
Deborah. "I know that she felt justified in her
actions. I still love my daughter absolutely. I am committed to doing whatever is necessary, without vio-
lating my integrity, for us to restore our relationship.
I want my daughter to forgive me for anything I did
that didn't work for her. I want my daughter whole,
and I want to have our relationship back."

Gonneke Spits spoke about this rather sad tale by
talking about what she called an interesting irony.
"Werner loved the opera. One of his favorites was
'Otello' written by Giuseppe Verdi. I don't know why
this particular opera was one of his favorites. Maybe
he had become interested in the story, which was
based on a Shakespeare play, because he had seen his
friend Raul Julia play the leading role in New York.
Werner also studied Shakespeare when he was younger," Spits said.[19]

"Otello became the classic example of how easy
it is for an upright person to be manipulated by their
high ideals and strong sense of justice into a position of destructive self-righteousness. In the story,
one piece of very questionable evidence was all it
took for Otello to make up his mind that the wife
he loved so much was guilty of infidelity and therefore deserved the ultimate punishment. He killed her
with his own hands. Of course Desdemona was not
guilty. Someone very close to Otello, to fill his own
needs, planted false evidence. He put Desdemona's
handkerchief in a place that would cause suspicion.
This flimsy piece of evidence was enough to distort
Otello's thinking in a way that kept him from seeing
all the signs, abundantly clear to the audience, that
his wife was not actually guilty. He could not hear
his wife's protestations of innocence. And while it
caused him great anguish, his sense of self-righteousness, and his sense that his trust in her was violated
overcame his love for his wife, and he killed her."

Erhard's children had many forces at work on them beyond not having a traditional father. They were subjected to news articles and rumors about their father over the years that portrayed him as a cult leader and charlatan. He refused to defend himself when especially controversial pieces hit the press. He trusted that his children would rely on their own experience and not be influenced by what others said. At family gatherings, the family would sometimes read the articles that had been written. Individual members of the family would share their experiences that were either contrary to or confirmed what was said. Of course, when something good was said about Erhard, that was shared with the family as well. He wanted them to know both sides of what would be present in the public conversation that they would surely bump into with their classmates and friends.

Although he didn't know it until much later, there were other pressures on his children to view him in a negative light. The web of those conspiring against Erhard also had a heavy influence on his children. Before Pimental appeared on *60 Minutes,* she and her sister were contacted by no less than seven of those who had joined forces to destroy Erhard.

Celeste Erhard told of her mother inviting her to come into the end of a long meeting she was having with Pimental and the accusing sister at her house a short time before Pimental decided to be interviewed by *60 Minutes.* Celeste said that her mother, Erhard's ex-wife, wanted her to hear an accusation being made by Celeste's half-sisters against her father. Ellen had her own axe to grind in the matter.[20]

Like some of his children, Erhard's second wife had a hard time living up to what they thought he expected of them. Ellen told Erhard's biographer that at one point "I felt like a dud, such a failure, next to him. I always knew he was extraordinary, but I

hadn't at first realized how extraordinary he was.
. . . I just couldn't keep up."[21] Early in their marriage, Erhard had a number of affairs which he later
readily admitted to his wife and even later reported
to his biographer.

Celeste thinks her mother never got over her
father's indiscretions. Even before her parents separated in 1982, Celeste remembers as a young child
her mother talking badly about her father. She said
her mother would tell her and her brother and sister lurid details about her sex life with Erhard. "I
was a pre-teenager and had no way of dealing with
that kind of information at that age. She was always
trying to turn us against Dad." And it worked for
a very long time. "I believed what my mother told
me, and it made me think my father was twisted and
evil. My reality became my mother's stories."[22]

Just after she appeared on *60 Minutes,* as a result
of professional counseling she had been receiving,
Celeste said she realized that she and her siblings had
been cunningly manipulated. Over the years, they
had been indoctrinated with a twisted picture of
their father that distorted even their personal
experience of him. Celeste found the strength and
courage to repair her relationship with her father,
but Celeste and her siblings weren't the only ones
who had been under Ellen's influence.

Pat Fry said that Ellen also worked on her four
children who, at various times, lived with Ellen for
short periods, especially in the first few years when
they moved from Philadelphia to the West Coast.
"When I found out, I was really angry," Fry said.
"I thought that was going too far. Her marriage had
nothing to do with me and my kids." Fry especially
remembers her son being upset at things Ellen would
tell him when he lived with her for a year.[23]

Spits said that life with Erhard was never easy for Ellen. "She was overwhelmed by all the activity and work going on around Werner. She really preferred the life of a housewife, but what she got was a powerhouse," Spits said. "Werner was growing every minute, making things happen—he was an extraordinary person. And it was an uncomfortable environment for Ellen. But you either played in the same league with Werner or you didn't. It was fine with him if you didn't want to play and you said you didn't—he was not one to try to make people into something they were not willing to be—but Ellen was never straight about it. She enjoyed the benefits of being an important part of Werner's exciting life, but didn't want to pay the price.

"Werner loved Ellen and his children," Spits said. "The children could just have easily said 'My life is so great because I have this father' instead of 'My life is so terrible because of my father.' But they were stuck in their own inability to live up to what they thought he expected of them," Spits said. "Perhaps one of the major ironies in Erhard's relationship with his children is that they were manipulated into seeing him as the manipulator. And I feel sad that Ellen didn't choose to have the great life she could have had with Werner instead of being so bitter and resentful about who he was in the world. It didn't have to go that way, and they didn't have to destroy Werner in the process."[24]

To understand the nature of the forces at work and the individual motivations which allowed some of Erhard's children to be used in the effort to destroy him, it is necessary to look back into the history of his family.

Although he had not intended to do so, Erhard started his own family when he was just 18 and still John Paul Rosenberg, fresh out of high school in

Philadelphia. He married his high school girlfriend, Pat Fry, in September 1953 and the following March their first daughter was born. The next year another daughter came along, followed by a son in 1958 and a third daughter in 1959. At 24, Erhard had four children and a wife to support which he did by working at various jobs during the six year period, mostly as a construction supervisor and later by selling automobiles. But apparently Erhard was bored and unhappy, domesticity didn't suit him. He felt trapped in his circumstances.

From the time he was a small child, Erhard had been intensely curious about life. He would sit for hours listening to his father discuss religion and the Bible with a friend who, like his father, had converted from Judaism to Christianity. Erhard pondered questions that many adults often find too overwhelming to even consider, much less dwell on.

"I wondered whether there really was a God, what all that I had been taught to believe in really meant. I wondered why God made it so bad? Why did he make war and famine? I also asked whether I was really responsible," Erhard told his biographer, the late philosopher, W.W. Bartley III, in the mid-1970s.[25]

By the time Erhard reached high school, his attention was already turned in a non-traditional direction. "I had begun to detach myself from my surroundings—from my family, my friends, my teachers. What was going on within removed me from the world around me. Nor was there anyone with whom I could talk about it," Erhard said in Bartley's biography of him.[26]

"I was interested in the problems of human existence, human relationship, love, sex, the purpose of it all, values, ethics, integrity. I could not discuss such things with my family.''[27]

In May 1960, six months after his fourth child was born, Erhard left the world that seemed to be closing in on him with June Bryde, a woman he had been seeing for over a year—his "ray of light," the person he felt he could talk to about his visions, his ideas and his philosophical questions. They changed their names to Werner and Ellen Erhard and headed west in search of the truth about life.

Erhard mastered the art of selling books, and was an executive in a couple of corporations while he also participated in numerous programs and disciplines over the next 10 years. In the process, he was creating his own training and development course which he actually put into place in October 1971 and called it the est Training. He had found what he was looking for. Almost a year later, in late 1972, Erhard returned to Philadelphia to clean up the mess he had created and left behind. By then, he and Ellen had three children—Celeste, 9; Adair, 8; and St. John, 4.

In the meantime after Erhard had been gone for five years, his first wife, Pat Fry, had married an old friend, Herb Campbell. She was in the process of divorcing Campbell when Erhard returned to his family in Philadelphia. The children never related to their step-father as a father. "We always knew that Dad was going to come home some day. We used to sit around and talk about it," said Lynn who was 5 when he left.[28]

To start the reconciliation process, Erhard first went to his parents, Joe and Dorothy Rosenberg. His mother had been devastated when he left, and her other three children had always thought that once Erhard came home—which they, too, knew he would—she'd be fine again. She was thrilled to see him and forgave him almost immediately, but said it took her husband a while to get over his anger at their son.[29] A few weeks after reuniting with his parents, Erhard came back to the Philadelphia area to see Pat.

Fry said she was shocked at how much she still felt for him when she saw him again—like he had never left. Although soft-spoken and mild-mannered, Fry is a very strong and independent person. She had not even told her parents that Erhard had left her and the children until months after he was gone. She found ways on her own to support them, including going on welfare for a while, until she could get a sewing business established. But despite the hardships she had endured in Erhard's absence, she too forgave him. She said she had known from the first day she laid eyes on him that he was going to accomplish great things in his life. And she knew that, from his perspective at the time he left, she and the children were keeping him from pursuing his dreams.[30]

Then, in the early part of 1973, Erhard met with his four children—it had been nearly 13 years since he left. They talked for hours in that initial meeting. He told them everything he had done and he answered all their questions. He then asked for their forgiveness—which everyone generously gave—and made arrangements to repay the people who had helped support his family in his absence. The last step was for the two families—Ellen and her children, Pat and her children—to meet. Although awkward, the meeting went smoothly.

Soon after the reconciliation, most of Erhard's family members in Philadelphia participated in the est Training and then relocated to the West Coast to be near and work with Erhard. His four older children, who had been adopted by Pat's husband, changed their last name to Erhard.

Erhard talked at length about his relationship with each of his older children. "I don't think my son ever fully forgave me for deserting my family. Until he went off to college, while he and I got along all right, it seemed to me that he kept himself at arms length. For the most part, I gave my children the chance to make their own decisions in life. I wanted them to grow up knowing that their life belonged to them, and that they were responsible for their own life."[31]

When each of his children graduated from high school, Erhard gave them a substantial sum of money and bought them a partnership interest in a successful business owned by a friend. He wanted to let them get on with their lives without any dependence. He told them that was their inheritance, and they didn't need to be nice to him so that he would include them in his will.

"My son dropped out of college and squandered all of the money," Erhard said. "While what he did was foolish, he was no fool. He had real strength of character." His son told Erhard that he wanted to learn more discipline and was going to join the Marines. "I was proud that my son was honest with himself. I admired his emerging maturity. But I was a little concerned about his using four years of his life at the best time for gaining an education." Although Erhard told his son he would learn the discipline the first six months and still have three and a half years to serve, his son went ahead and enlisted.

"While I wasn't sure that he made the right choice, I respected his decision," Erhard said. "I couldn't help but admire the guts it took to make that choice." His son, although not particularly happy during some of the experience, really made the best of it and came out having been promoted a number of times and with a very successful record. He then became a full-time student, accepting Erhard's standing offer to all his children to support them with their education at any time. Erhard said that after graduating early, his son went to Hawaii to start his own business.

"It was around this time that his sister told him that I had raped her. As I said, I found this out when she called and told me her brother had made that up. When I called my son to find out what was going on, he told me what his sister had actually said. I could understand his outrage. I told him that the accusation was false, and that he, his sisters, his mother and I should all get together to get it resolved. I told him that there was nothing I could say, without his sister being present, that would convince him that the accusation was false."

Erhard told me that the meeting was difficult for everyone present, and that it was impossible to resolve the accusation because at the last minute, the daughter who had made the accusation decided not to come. "I set up the meeting because I trusted that in my presence my daughter would tell the truth. But she was not present, and the whole point of the meeting was gone for me. Because of that, during the meeting, I was primarily concerned that I not say anything that would make it more difficult for her to tell the truth later. I couldn't counter the accusation without calling my daughter a liar and I wasn't willing to do that. I suppose I could have attacked my daughter, but I knew it would only serve to get her stuck in her position, and make it more difficult for her whenever she was willing to be with us all and tell the truth. I told the family that I was not going to speak for my daughter, that I wanted her to have the opportunity to speak for herself."

"At the meeting, my son at first was particularly harsh. Apparently the children had all met with their sister prior to the meeting, and she told them the

story in a very convincing way. By the time my son
got to the meeting, he was convinced that every act
of support for my children and every expression of
love and even all of the normal, everyday interac-
tions parents have with their children were all somehow a manipulation on my part. The children had
apparently reached a consensus on how I was as a
father. They were all saying the same things in the
same words. They reinterpreted all the years of my
support of them and my expressions of affection for
them as nothing more than an attempt on my part
to win them over and to look good in public. They
took every instance of my being straight with them
and called it being bad with them."

Erhard said his former wife, Pat Fry, commented
during the meeting that she thought the children's
accusations were unfair. But for the most part, she
remained silent to give the children the chance to
have their say. "For most of the meeting, instead of
addressing the accusation, the meeting became an
attempt by the children to get me clear that there
was something wrong with me," Erhard said. "Of
course, I could understand their anger, given my
daughter's accusation, which without thinking
about, they would have no reason to doubt. It
seemed that they had all adopted Deborah's slant on
me when they met privately with their sister, before
the meeting with their mother and me. I thought that
the anger and resentment that they were now all
expressing about our relationship was a product of
trying to get their experience of me in the past to
match the accusation made by their sister. I was trying to get them to see that the past had to be pretty
badly distorted to make that even conceivable."

The meeting continued late into the night. Erhard
said, "Between all the back and forth, I tried to
remind my family about the years that I had nur-

tured that daughter and took care of her. I asked them to remember their own observations of her relationship with me which was so entirely inconsistent with the idea that I could have raped her. The two just didn't fit together. I felt that was all I could say to give my family some access to the truth, and at the same time not get my other daughter stuck with her fabrication.

"After hours of going around and around I got clear that none of the facts were going to make any difference in resolving the accusation, as long as they believed I raped their sister. I decided that while I wanted my daughter to have the chance to tell the truth about it herself, I had to say something at this meeting about the accusation. I said, 'I am still not going to speak for [the daughter who made the accusation] but I want to be clear that no such thing ever happened. I never had intercourse with my daughter.' I told the family that I was not going to address the accusation further than that, because I wanted my daughter to have the chance to tell the truth about it herself when she found the strength to do that," Erhard said.

"Some of those present came to the meeting already doubting the accusation, but at first they were confused by my refusal to say outright that the accusation was a lie. When I finally said what I was willing to say without my daughter being present, I think that Pat, Lynn and her brother believed what I said, but Deborah never did. But because I didn't speak about it further, some of them may have been left with the false impression that while I didn't rape my daughter, and didn't have intercourse with her, I was saying that something happened."

Erhard said at the end of the meeting, he walked out to the parking lot with his son. "I had the sense that even though the issue was a long way from being resolved, my son was beginning to have at least some doubts about its veracity. I said, 'Look son, given your sister's refusal to discuss the accusation, I have no way of proving the truth of what I told you, but I'm willing to go with you and take a lie detector test.' He said that wasn't necessary.''

Erhard did eventually take a lie detector test and provided his son a copy of it. "We had some short discussions about the accusation and I think that he spoke with his sister at length. In any case, it's my impression that by now my son at least had serious doubts about the truthfulness of his sister's allegation. He and I are in decent communication. We seem to be speaking to each other based on our experience of each other, rather than on what anyone else has said about either one of us. My son has had to be a very big man throughout all of this. I respect his willingness to hear the other side, when hearing the other side is almost impossible. By the same token, I know that he loves his sister and wants to support her and isn't willing to make her wrong.''

Although she had to resolve some issues of her own, Erhard's second daughter Lynn has remained supportive of her father. "When I reunited with my family, Lynn was in her late teens but was already somewhat a woman of the world. For some reason she was less sheltered than the other children, and had a certain early maturity.

She had gotten into some trouble as a teenager. When she came out to the West Coast, she participated in a 10-day residential program we offered for teens and she used that program to put the past in the past and create a new spectrum of possibilities for her life.''

Lynn decided she wanted to be a professional hairdresser and was trained at Vidal Sassoon. Erhard said she was very successful in her career. "However, she came to me and said, 'I have a great job, I make good money, and I have wonderful friends. But I want to make a difference in life, and without a formal education, I feel limited in doing that. I want to go to college.' I told Lynn that after being out in the world, particularly after being so successful in her work, going to college and living as a student would be difficult. But I admired her willingness to give that up to do what she needed to prepare herself to make a difference." Erhard told her that if she was really committed to going to college, he would pay her way and support her, the same offer to support any amount of education he made to all his children. "I was so proud of Lynn. I was well aware of the strength of character that it took for a person not to be stuck with a life that, while very successful, was not truly fulfilling. I admired her commitment to live a life that made a difference," Erhard said.

"In my universe, Lynn was a star. She was savvy about life, very well grounded, knew what she wanted, was willing to pay the price to get it, didn't make excuses, or try to justify her actions, and had real integrity. She graduated from Mills College with honors and started her career in the computer field with a company working on leading edge technology." Erhard said that Lynn has been promoted many times during her career, every time to jobs with more responsibility.

"While Lynn has no pretensions of being a sophisticated thinker, she's a woman with good judgement," Erhard said. "She's always been her own person, not letting anybody do her thinking for her. She has been a voice of reason in this whole mess, not taking any one side. Lynn has maintained her commitment to an authentic resolution of this affair, even when others were completely stuck in their position, or got tired of getting at the truth, or found the situation hopeless." Erhard said he was grateful to her for her stabilizing influence and her maturity. "I'm pleased that she has looked to take care of everyone."

While Erhard spoke with compassion, love, and respect for each of his children, it was obvious that his first wife had a very special place in his heart. He clearly thought she was special and was devoted to her. "One of the things I hate most about all of this, is the impact it has had on Pat. It has disturbed her profoundly, created difficult conflicts for her, and left her troubled. I think she's gotten to the point where, while she desperately wants to see it resolved, she finds it so distasteful she feels the need to avoid it. It's not too much to say Pat is a saint. I always loved Pat, but as I matured I came to appreciate her more and more. She's a woman of great strength of character who has always done what she could to nurture the people in her life. When given the chance to choose resentment rather than forgiveness, she chose to forgive, even when there was every reason to resent.

"If it had not been for her generosity and magnanimity, I could never have successfully reunited with my family. Reuniting with my family was one of the most important turning points in my life. I'm deeply grateful to Pat, and love her for who she is. I'm really sorry to have been involved in any way in something which caused her grief. She truly deserves nothing but joy."

Finally Erhard came to talk about the daughter who had accused him of raping her. In my interview with him, Erhard seemed completely natural and at ease. He seemed to be doing nothing more than saying what was there for him, and he was obviously comfortable doing that. However, when he began to speak about this daughter, I thought I detected a note of sadness.

Erhard told me that he had always identified with this daughter and had a certain compassion for her. He said he too had made a mess of his early life and had to struggle to turn himself around. He told me he had a lot of respect for her because he felt she had been doing just that for the three years before she cut off all contact with him. She had divorced her third husband, and Erhard was supporting her so that she could both go back to school and raise her young son. From all reports, they spoke frequently, they spent as much time together as they could, and she was assisting him in his work. He said she had decided not to get into another relationship right away, she wanted to try life without someone to lean on. He told me that it was hard for her, and maybe a little frightening, but that she stuck with it. He said that she finished school, had started working as an apprentice, that the period where they had agreed he would support her was nearing its end, and soon she would begin being fully on her own.

Erhard said that, while there would be one more phone call, the last time he saw his daughter was when she accompanied him to a dinner given for the then-speaker of the house, Jim Wright. "She really enjoyed herself at that dinner. The people at her table thought she was wonderful and on the way out stopped and told me so. We had a good time on the way home. We laughed together about her having been worried about being able to relate with the kind of people who would be at the dinner. She was proud and pleased at the way she had handled herself. She told me she would now like to be invited even more often to those kinds of opportunities."

A few days after the dinner, Erhard left on a long

overseas trip. By the time he got back, his daughter
had quit work and moved in with a man. Erhard told
me that the last time he talked to his daughter was
after he returned from the trip, on the phone call
where she told him that her brother had somehow
come up with the idea that her father had raped her.
While Erhard made numerous attempts to be in
touch with his daughter, to this day, she has not been
willing to talk to him.

The family had a tradition of addressing family
issues in an open meeting. Fry and Erhard set up a
meeting between the four children and themselves
to give the family a chance to address the accusation and resolve the truth about it together. Fry said
that she invited the daughter who made the accusation to come to the meeting and given that her mother, her brother, and her two sisters would be present,
she agreed. However Fry told me that at the very
last minute she backed out of the meeting she had
agreed to come to. Fry and Erhard were stunned
when she didn't come.

It seems that no one in the family except Pimental still believes the accusation that Erhard raped his
daughter. Pimental's brother was understandably
outraged when he first heard the accusation. However, as a result of what he heard at the family meeting and the outcome of Erhard's lie detector test,
and whatever other inconsistencies he noticed, her
brother apparently also came to doubt the truth of
the accusation. In fact, he cut off his relationship
with Pimental after she went on *60 Minutes* and
made their sister's accusation public.

Not one of the many family members, and those
close to the family, who were interviewed, said they
believed the accusation. Many of them cited circumstances in the accusing daughter's history which
would indicate that the accusation was a fabrication.

According to family members, she never mentioned or even hinted that she had been in any way sexually abused by her father until nine years after she claimed it had happened. During those nine years, the daughter gave no evidence that she had anything but an entirely normal relationship with her father. They were mostly close, and Erhard was supportive of her in many ways. She apparently reciprocated by frequently demonstrating her own support and respect for her father. Like any normal family, they also had their differences.[32]

There was one serious fallout between them when this daughter would not cease a relationship with a man who had given Erhard concern for his daughter's safety. I heard a lot about Erhard's relationship with this daughter, but not one of the reports was consistent with her accusation.

The daughter claiming to have been raped told her siblings it happened when she was on a trip with Erhard. She said her uncle, Harry Rosenberg, and Maxine Forbes, Erhard's assistant at the time, were on the same trip. Forbes worked for Erhard until 1985. In her 1992 sworn statement, Forbes said, "I have known [the daughter who claimed the rape] for most of her adult life, and can attest to the fact that she has been known to exaggerate and fabricate things and to lie, and when confronted face to face with the truth, she has a tendency to stick to her guns even when the evidence to the contrary is indisputable.

"I can also attest to the often close and supportive nature of the relationship between [this daughter] and her father throughout the time I was employed by Werner. She had always been able to ask for her father's support and took advantage of that whenever she had problems, which occurred frequently. Even when Werner did not always agree with her personal choices and decisions, he always unequivocally supported her in whatever way he could. If such a serious event had occurred between the two of them, I am certain that she would have exhibited at least some change in her relationship with her father after that event. I can say absolutely that there was no change in the quality of her relationship with her father during the period of time in question. ... As [she] claims that I was present during this one trip where she claims to have been raped, I would certainly have noticed either some diminished relatedness with her father, or some discomfort on her part, and I noticed none, whatsoever."[33]

Gonneke Spits, having known his family intimately since the mid-1960s, said that particular daughter had a "huge fantasy life." Spits said she was prone to blow everything out of perspective. "For example, when her young son had a runny nose, she came to me wanting to see her father convinced that her son had pneumonia. She would make things up out of something that wasn't much of anything."[34]

Spits said she doesn't know why that daughter turned on her father. "When she was close to Werner, they were very close," said Spits. "They were good friends. They worked well together, did things together. She openly showed a tremendous amount of love and affection for her father, but she also took advantage of the situation.

"You know, one of the problems with Werner I've always said is, 'he's too good for his own good'. He was very generous with his kids, always supporting them in whatever they were doing. And she was constantly asking for more support—she'd go to school, drop out, get married, get divorced, go back to school, etc.

"She had a lot of heart though. I really wish that she had stayed with her commitment to participate with her father because when she did, she was very happy and they worked well together," Spits said.

To her credit, the accusing daughter refused to surrender to the pressure of the conspiracy to make her accusation public. Erhard would only say the following about his daughter and what her allegation did to him: "I still believe that it's possible for her and me to be in communication. I'm committed to working this out with her. I know my daughter, and I trust that one day she will want to set the record straight for herself."

[1] Kathy Cronkite, "Jack & Debby Erhard: The Est Family," 1977, p. 177.

[2] The Brannso School yearbook, 1977.

[3] John Hubner, "Est founder's daughter says Erhard molested her, raped her sister," *San Jose Mercury News,* March 3, 1991.

[4] Interview with Pat Fry, February 22, 1922.

[5] Transcript and videotape of *60 Minutes* program, March 3,1991.

[6] Interview with Pat Fry, February 22, 1992.

[7] Interview with Pat Fry, February 22, 1922.

[8] Transcript and videotape of *60 Minutes,* March 3, 1991.

[9] Statement by Lynn Erhard, undated.

[10] Interview with Werner Erhard, September 15, 1991.

[11] Interview with Pat Fry, February 22, 1992.

[12] Interview with Lynn Erhard, January 2, 1992.

[13] Interview with Gonneke Spits, June 5, 1992.

[14] Interview with Werner Erhard, September 15, 1991.

[15] Interview with Lynn Erhard, January 2, 1992.

[16] Interview with Werner Erhard, September 15, 1991.

[17] Interview with Pat Fry, February 22, 1992.

[18] Interview with Werner Erhard, September 15, 1991.

[19] Interview with Gonneke Spits, June 5, 1992.

[20] Interview with Celeste Erhard, February 22, 1992.

[21] Bartley, p. 139.

[22] Interview with Celeste Erhard, February 22, 1992.

[23] Interview with Pat Fry, February 22, 1992.

[24] Interview with Gonneke Spits, June 5, 1992.

[25] Bartley, p. 14.

[26] Bartley, p. 27.

[27] Bartley, p. 28.

[28] Interview with Lynn Erhard, January 2, 1992.

[29] Interview with Dorothy Rosenberg, December 30, 1991.

[30] Interview with Pat Fry, February 22, 1992.

[31] Interview with Werner Erhard, September 15, 1991.

[32] Interviews with Dorothy Rosenberg, December 30, 1991; Nathan Rosenberg, January 1, 1992; Joan Rosenberg, December 31, 1992; Jayne Sillari, December 28, 1991; Lynn Erhard, January 2, 1991; Harry Rosenberg, February 1, 1922; Celeste Erhard, February 22, 1992; Pat Fry, February 22, 1992; Gonneke Spits, June 5, 1992; Laurel Scheaf, June 5, 1992.

[33] Sworn affidavit by Maxine Forbes, 1992.

[34] Interview with Gonneke Spits, June 5, 1992.

CHAPTER VII
THE MEDIA IMAGE

Well before *60 Minutes* destroyed Erhard's reputation, controversy seemed to follow him. Werner
Erhard was a unique individual and not easily understood, especially by members of the press who often
interpreted his confidence as arrogance. He was one
of those people the press loved to hate. He was successful, popular, confident, intense, self-educated,
straightforward, and honest. Early in his career, he
publicly acknowledged that he had abandoned a wife
and four children and that he had been involved in
affairs during both of his marriages. His life was an
open book that he readily shared with thousands of
people.[1]

Erhard almost never spoke of his accomplishments. Consequently, few people—other than those
who read his 1978 biography—ever knew that he
was the general manager of an industrial equipment
company and the vice president of a major international corporation, both before he was 30. Journal-

ists giving background on Erhard almost always referred to him as a former used car salesman. While not inaccurate—Erhard did sell automobiles before he left his family in Philadelphia—it was certainly an incomplete, one-dimensional picture of him.

Erhard discovered early how easily his words could be taken out of context or misunderstood and how easily his work could be misinterpreted. When Sharon Spaulding became director of media relations for Werner Erhard and Associates (WE&A) in 1985, she said she was constantly having to correct errors that were made in the media in the early 1970s, errors that were perpetuated by journalists building on that as background information.[2]

Those errors may very well have been the result of the Church of Scientology's campaign to discredit Erhard in the press, a campaign which was launched shortly after Erhard founded the *est* Training in 1971 and reported on in a 1979 *Denver Post*[3] article and later in the December 29, 1991 *Los Angeles Times*.[4] The *Post* article described the FBI's 1977 raid of the Scientology headquarters in Los Angeles and Washington, D.C., which revealed Scientology's plot to frame author Paulette Cooper with criminal activities, as well as the campaign to destroy Erhard.

While the extent of Scientology's early campaign is unknown, the image of Erhard which began to emerge by the mid-70s was that of a cult leader and greedy exploiter of the public with kooky, half-baked programs in pop psychology. It is known—according to what one of Scientology's hired agents, Ted Heisig, told the *Los Angeles Times*—that Jesse Kornbluth, the author of one of the first major attacks on Erhard, was in direct contact with Roger Stodola, an executive of the church.

According to Spaulding, Erhard didn't help his

image in the press—at least, not in the beginning. "When the Training first started, it took off much faster than anyone thought possible. There was an enormous demand for the Training, and the attention of the organization was on meeting that demand, not on communicating with the press," said Spaulding, who also said there were a lot of mistakes made in those days when dealing with the press.

"Werner made no effort to describe the programs in a way that made sense. Therefore, he ended up an easy target for the media. After the first few negative articles, Werner felt burned by the press and retreated rather than have free dialogue with members of the press," said Spaulding.[5]

Erhard and the people around him were cautious about Erhard granting interviews to journalists, although he certainly continued to do so. Kornbluth referred to that caution as "harassment and intimidation" in his 1976 feature story in *New Times*, "The Fuhrer Over *est*," a scathing piece about Erhard and his work.[6]

For the next decade and a half, the *New Times* article was followed by numerous other negative, derogatory stories about Erhard and his work. In the meantime, Erhard and his company had matured in their relationship with the press. Erhard had established an open-door policy with the press by the late 1970s and was committed to being accessible and have other members of the staff available for interviews. But reporters and writers continued to depend on previously printed information on Erhard for background, assuming it to be true, and then based their current stories on that distorted image. NEXIS, a computerized information retrieval service, often used for research, provides easy access to articles published in certain magazines and newspapers. In addition to Kornbluth's article, a NEXIS search would find titles such as "Bad Vibes From *Est*," "Let Them Eat *Est*," "What Has *Est* Done For Us Lately?," "How *Est* Didn't Change My Life," "You Are What You *Est*," "In the Wake of TM and Zen, a Former Encyclopedia Huckster is the Smooth Guru of *Est*," and many more.[7] All articles about Erhard and his work were not negative, but those which were neutral or positive were usually overlooked and not used for reference.

Spaulding said she often received telephone calls from reporters who said they were on deadline and wanted a quick comment from her. She'd later learn that the reporter had been working on the story for weeks, and even months, and had only made the call in order to appear as if the information was balanced and objective. When she had sufficient notice of a pending story and the opportunity to provide information to reporters, Spaulding said many reporters "eventually decided not to do their story because they realized there wasn't a story to do when they got all the facts."[8] But it didn't always work that way.

In 1985, Richard Behar and Ralph King Jr., wrote an article for *Forbes* magazine about Erhard's finances, specifically the transactions that took place when he established WE&A as a sole proprietorship in 1981. In the first paragraph Erhard was called the "millionaire guru of *est* who began life as Jack Rosenberg of Philadelphia and who once sold used cars for a living." The article was filled with factual inaccuracies about the complicated process that Erhard had gone through with the companies he founded. It was presented in such a way as to make Erhard look like a conniving operative hiding his assets.[9] For example, the article stated that a $15 million dollar loan Erhard acquired to buy the assets of *est*, an educational corporation, the company which previously offered the courses Erhard designed but which Erhard never owned, was used as a "key prop in Erhard's empire, which stretches across 20 countries and a bewildering array of foundations, trusts and tax haven shells." There was a complex financial structure which is explained in the next chapter, but Erhard never had an empire of foundations and trusts. He had no ownership in any of the organizations referred to in the article. When Behar and King were preparing the piece, Werner Erhard and Associates offered to the *Forbes* editors any information they needed to report the facts accurately and in fact, did provide that information. It was not used. The *Forbes* article also became part of the NEXIS file.

Erhard was often called a guru and his work a cult. A 1984 *People Weekly* story about his pending divorce from Ellen Erhard said he "was a guru's guru."[10] A 1989 *Philadelphia Inquirer* article called Erhard the "erstwhile God-King of *est*."[11] Even articles which were not totally negative picked up on the terminology like Mark MacNamara's 1988 story for *Los Angeles Magazine* which was titled "The Return of Werner Erhard: Guru II."[12]

Occasionally, a publication would print a retraction when its hand was called. A London publication printed an article in March 1988, "Could you be seduced by sects appeal?," which claimed *est* and other programs with which Erhard was associated were cults. As a result of a suit filed by Erhard against the magazine, in September 1989 it published an apology and full retraction plus paid the legal fees for the suit.[13]

Although there was never anything to join, no creed or doctrine to believe in, cult watchdogs branded Erhard's work a cult saying it practiced mind-control and brainwashing. The Cult Awareness

Network is a loose-knit confederation of parents'
groups, deprogrammers, dissatisfied former group
members of various cults, mental health profession-
als, attorneys, and evangelical groups—all concerned
about keeping youth from being brainwashed or
otherwise influenced by cults operating outside
traditional religious and spiritual avenues.[14] This
movement, although started by people with good
intentions, became particularly hostile in the early
'80s to anything that smacked of "new age." They
decided that Erhard was playing God and preach-
ing beliefs that rob people of their values, morals and
dignity—despite the fact that studies have shown
that none of Erhard's programs interfere with people's religious beliefs and despite the fact that some
of the country's most respected members of the
clergy have participated in those programs and even
designed their own course and non-profit organization based on their participation.

Representatives of the Cult Awareness Network,
particularly its director Cynthia Kisser, are often
quoted by journalists as experts on Erhard's "cult."
In turn, a call to the network's headquarters asking
for information on Erhard, *est*, or the Forum, along
with $10, will net the caller 64 photocopied pages
of many of the published newspaper and magazine
articles which portray Erhard in a negative light and
a reference list of other articles and books which
negatively describe Erhard.

Another often-quoted "expert" on cults and
Erhard is Margaret Singer, a psychologist working
in the area of anti-cultism since the late 1970s.
Although Singer had done no scientific studies on
est or the Forum, she was frequently called on as an
expert witness against Erhard—in the press, the
courts, and divorce proceedings. Her testimony was
ruled inadmissible in one case. The court order said

she "cannot support her opinion with testimony that involves thought reform, because the court finds that her views on thought reform, like Dr. Ofshe's (Richard Ofshe, another 'expert') are not generally accepted within the scientific community." While being deposed for a personal injury suit against Erhard, Singer had to admit that *est* was not a cult.[16]

According to an affidavit from Scientology's agent Ted Heisig, the now disaffected participant of Erhard's programs, Paul Gutfreund, and Scientology executive Roger Stodola, used journalists to print what they fed them. Heisig said that Gutfreund was in regular, sometimes daily communication with Don Lattin of the *San Francisco Chronicle* and had four or five other reporters he was talking to. Gutfreund told Heisig that he had gone to a television reporter in San Francisco and that he had contacted CBS's "60 Minutes."[17]

Heisig also said one of his supervisors, Roger Stodola, had fed information to John Hubner of the *San Jose Mercury News*; Jonathan Littman, an author who reportedly was doing a piece on Erhard; and Richard Behar, who reportedly was writing an article for *Time* magazine.[18]

A group of over 200 former employees were so frustrated by the inaccurate and distorted picture the press presented of what it was like working with Erhard, particularly the article that appeared in the November issue of *San Francisco Focus Magazine*, that they put together an ad in response, paying for it out of their own pockets. The ad said that their former company was a great place to work, and that they had enjoyed and benefitted from their experience of working there. Two San Francisco publications refused to even accept their ad which was attempting to set the record straight before it was finally printed in the *San Francisco Chronicle*. None of these hundreds of employees and former employees whose view of working with Erhard was so contradictory of what was being said in the press was ever interviewed.

"*Focus* never tried to get interviews from anybody on staff," Spaulding said. "We even went over there and provided information about everything, including financial statements. It was all ignored."[19]

Shortly after the *Focus* article, the *San Jose Mercury News* series by John Hubner appeared and included some comments by Hubert Dreyfus, a professor of philosophy at UC-Berkeley. On November 18, Dreyfus sent a letter to the editor of the *News* saying he was distressed that his comments were "used out of context so as to appear to support critical allegations concerning the personality of Werner Erhard and the culture of his company, WE&A."[20] That letter was never published.

Most of the articles which appeared during 1990 were based on the Afremow case and painted Erhard as an abusive employer living an eccentric, excessive lifestyle with the funds he milked from his own company. Then in November 1990, with Hubner's scathing series on Erhard, members of Erhard's family became involved with the media.

When *60 Minutes* reported that Erhard had raped his daughter, the media image of him was complete. His reputation was destroyed. There was nothing left to accuse him of other than murder. While quick to jump on the sensationalism about Erhard, there was rarely any attempt to report a balanced view. Long-time employees who enjoyed working with him, participants who found value in his programs, and executives who knew the facts about the business were not heard from. And the attack doesn't seem to have yet run its course.

In late 1991 legal reporter, Steven Pressman, approached Spaulding, who had left WE&A after her second child was born in early 1990 but was still often sought out for information on Erhard. He informed her he had a contract with St. Martin's Press to write a book about Erhard. He claimed to be just an honest writer out to tell the real biography of Werner Erhard. He told Spaulding that he had an agent in New York who secured the contract with St. Martin's for him. Perhaps, not so coincidentally, St. Martin's Press is the same publishing company which published Scientology's founder, L. Ron Hubbard's best-selling book *Battleship Earth* in 1982. Pressman has denied having any relationship with Scientology.

According to Spaulding, as of her last conversation with Pressman, his book is apparently going to be just another piece about Erhard's drive for money and fame. Sources close to Erhard say they do not believe Pressman was ever going to do a balanced and fair book on Erhard.

The power of the press—both print and electronic broadcast— has become a major concern for a lot of people. In the book *And That's The Way It Isn't: A Reference Guide to Media Bias*, former U.S. Ambassador to the United Nations Jeane Kirkpatrick wrote about her concerns in the foreword. "New powers have arisen: among them, the power of the media. Some people believe, and I am among them, that the power of the media today constitutes the most significant exercise of unaccountable power in our society. It is unaccountable to anyone, except for those who exercise the power. I believe that the domain of culture is as important as the domain of government or the economy. . . . No domain is more important than the domain in which the media operate. . . . It is very important to realize that the electronic media, which provide mass audiences, have made our culture much more manipulable than it ever was in the past."[22]

The press has played a powerful and important role in society. The uncovering of this century's worst political scandal, the third-rate burglary of Democratic headquarters in the Watergate Office Building, is a good example. However, Larry Martz who was *Newsweek*'s national affairs editor during the Watergate period, thinks journalists learned the wrong lessons from Watergate. "Watergate marked the era of celebrity journalism," Martz wrote in the June 22, 1992, *Newsweek*, which ran a special 20-year retrospective. "A generation of reporters saw themselves as Robert Redford and Dustin Hoffman, playing an idealized Bob Woodward and Carl Bernstein (the *Washington Post* reporters who broke the Watergate story in 1972), bagging a presidential head as a trophy on the wall," Martz wrote.[23]

"Watergate also taught us to trivialize. Presidents were to be impeached for high crimes and misdemeanors, which the Founding Fathers never got around to defining, but we in the media connived at reducing that grand concept to a legalistic search for smoking guns, a shabby procession of clowns testifying about schemes to catch Democrats with prostitutes or steal their psychiatric records."

In Carl Bernstein's reflections of post-Watergate journalism which appeared in the June 8, 1992, issue of *The New Republic*, he wrote: "For more than fifteen years we (journalists) have been moving away from real journalism toward the creation of a sleazoid info-tainment culture. . . . In this new culture of journalistic titillation, we teach our readers and our viewers that the trivial is significant, that the lurid and the loopy are more important than real news. We do not serve our readers and viewers, we pander to them. And we condescend to them, giving them what we think they want and what we calculate will sell and boost ratings and readership.

"What is happening today, unfortunately," continued Bernstein, "is that the lowest form of popular culture—lack of information, misinformation, disinformation, and a contempt for the truth or the reality of most people's lives—has overrun real journalism."[24]

For the most part, real journalism has been missing consistently in the media's coverage of Erhard, his work and his family. Even the complex intricacies of Erhard's business enterprises became fodder for the press, which never could quite get the full accurate picture.

[1] From Bartley, *Werner Erhard.*

[2] Interview with Sharon Spaulding, June 21, 1992.

[3] "Scientologist Plot Revealed," *Denver Post,* November 25, 1979.

[4] Welkos, *Los Angeles Times,* December 29, 1991.

[5] Interview with Sharon Spaulding, June 21, 1992.

[6] Jesse Kornbluth, "Fuhrer over est," *New Times,* March 19, 1976.

[7] Customized Database Survey & Literature Search, March 10, 1990.

[8] Interview with Sharon Spaulding, June 21, 1992.

[9] *Richard Behar and Ralph King Jr., "The Winds of Werner," Forbes,* 11/18/85.

[10] Marie Wilhem, "His wife and former followers question the human potential of est guru Werner Erhard," *People Weekly,* September 24, 1984

[11] Mary Lois Polak, "Werner Erhard did EST Create Uppies? No, says the Founder, that's Another Misinterpretation. And he's Mellowed now. He'll Let You go to the John," *Philadelphia Inquirer,* December 31, 1989.

[12] Mark MacNamara, "The Return of Werner Erhard: Guru II," *Los Angeles Magazine,* May, 1988.

[13] Press release from Werner Erhard and Associates, September 30, 1989.

[14] Lowell Streiker, Ph.D., "The Anticult Network," 1988.

[15] United States v. Stephen Fishman, U.S. District Court Northern District of California, March 15, 1990.

[16] Deposition of Margaret T. Singer, Ph.D., Alfrieda Slee, Admx of the estate of Jack Slee v. Werner Erhard et al, United States District Court District of Connecticut, p. 378.

[17] Affidavit by Ted Heisig, October 29, 1991.

[18] Affidavit by Ted Heisig, October 29, 1991.

[19] Interview with Sharon Spaulding, June 21, 1992.

[20] Letter from Hubert L. Dreyfus to Jeffrey Klein, editor, *San Jose Mercury News,* November 18, 1990.

[21] Interview with Sharon Spaulding, June 21, 1992.

[22] *And That's The Way It Isn't: A Reference Guide To Media Bias,* Edited by L. Brent Bozell III and Brent H. Baker. Foreword by Jeane Kirkpatrick. (Alexandria, Va.: Media Research Center, 1990), page xii.

[23] Larry Martz, "For the Media, a Pyrrhic Victory," *Newsweek,* June 22, 1992, p. 32.

[24] Carl Bernstein, "The Idiot Culture," *The New Republic,* June 8, 1992, p. 25.

CHAPTER VIII
MINDING ERHARD'S BUSINESS

Members of the press who played on the cynicism of the general public tried to prove that the person Werner Erhard claimed to be, who his associates and friends knew him to be, and who the nature of his work showed him to be, in fact, was devious and greedy. They were trying to portray him as someone who wasn't really committed to making a difference for people. They were saying he couldn't actually be interested in serving people or providing opportunities for others to make their lives work better. He must be "in it for the money." They tried to fit Erhard inside of a stereotype of preconceived notions.

Erhard's detractors created their "proof" from the complex structures of the various companies, especially the earlier ones, through which his programs were made available. Sprinkled throughout the media blitz of 1990-1991 were articles supposedly reporting on Erhard's legal battles with the Internal

Revenue Service. What the press made into a case of "tax evasion," "tax dodging," and "sham financial transactions to avoid taxes"[1] was really nothing more than a case of the IRS challenging certain business deductions Erhard had claimed in the early 1980s and Erhard disagreeing with the findings.[2] To those who based their view of Erhard on the constant stream of negative press, the simple truth that he was suing the IRS, and not at all being pursued by the agency, was inconceivable. This was, in fact, the situation. Erhard was never accused by the IRS of anything illegal. He was simply involved in a complex dispute with the IRS and was merely one of hundreds of taxpayers, both individuals and corporations, who each year bring lawsuits to challenge the IRS disallowance of legitimate business deductions.

Contrary to speculations and reports, Erhard never intended to amass inordinate wealth through the companies that were set up to deliver his programs. In fact, the companies were deliberately established so that neither he nor anyone else could gain great profit. He did, however, intend to live well, to have his family taken care of, and to be free to do what he wanted to do—design programs and train people.

In order to understand the truth about any alleged misdeeds of Erhard's, it's necessary to wade through boring, tedious and hard to understand material, almost all of which is public record in Erhard's tax case. A succession of four different companies have offered Erhard's programs to the public, only one of which he owned. The first, *Erhard Seminars Training, Inc.*, was established in September 1971. It was followed in September 1975 by *est, an educational corporation*. In 1981 Erhard formed his own company, not a corporation, but a sole proprietorship, named Werner Erhard and Associates.

Werner Erhard & Associates (WE&A) ceased doing business in February 1991. Erhard sold the assets used to operate the business, and granted a license to deliver the programs he had designed, to a company named Landmark Education Corporation which was formed by his former employees.

The first two of the four companies, *Erhard Seminars Training, Inc. (EST, Inc.)* and *est, an educational corporation (est, a.e.c.)*, were not owned by Erhard. He was a salaried employee of each of these companies. All of the stock of the first company was owned by International Aesthetics, Ltd. (IAL), a Nevada corporation. All of the stock of the second company was owned by a charitable trust named The Werner Erhard Charitable Settlement, domiciled in the Channel Islands of Jersey. Erhard had no control, ownership, or other interest in either IAL or The Werner Erhard Charitable Settlement. In fact, the charter of the Charitable Settlement provided that he could receive no benefits from the charity.[3]

WE&A, the third company in the line, was an unincorporated association, and Erhard was the sole proprietor. The present company offering Erhard's programs, Landmark Education Corporation (LEC), is entirely owned by the employees of the company. Erhard has no ownership interest or control, and is not connected with the company in any way.

While in the beginning the revenues in the succession of companies started small, they grew rapidly and at their peak in 1988, the annual revenues were $36 million. The staff also expanded rapidly and, in a very few years, went from a handful to hundreds of employees in various locations around the world. As the business grew, professional executives were hired to manage the companies.

Erhard had no ownership of *EST, Inc., est, a.e.c.,*

or any of the organizations which owned them and didn't control the finances or cash flow, but he did have control over the work done. "I had the kind of control a key employee of any company has," Erhard said. "The success or failure of the company depended largely on my performance. I was busy leading programs, giving talks in public, developing new programs, and training people so that there were others in addition to myself who could lead the courses. I didn't have much time left over to actually participate in the business end of the enterprise, but I made whatever contribution I could. I had complete control over the design and delivery of the programs. Before the professional executives were hired to run the company, I mostly decided who would work for the company and even afterward, I was at least consulted on the hiring of other key employees."[4]

In 1980 the IRS disallowed deductions that the first two companies had claimed on their tax returns for licensing fees and interest payments made on loans. The companies sued the IRS in U.S. Tax Court in an attempt to force the IRS to recognize the deductions. In 1986, the Tax Court ruled in favor of the IRS deciding that the transactions on which the deductions were based were tax motivated. The court awarded the IRS the taxes due on the disallowed deductions, plus interest and penalties. At the trial, Erhard testified for the IRS on what he knew regarding the transactions involved. He did not stand to gain or lose by the outcome of the trial because he had no ownership interest or control of the companies involved in the transactions. By the time of the trial, he was no longer even employed by the companies, and they were no longer delivering his programs. Erhard had long since started his own business, WE&A.

In 1985, Erhard's own company, WE&A, began to have its own problems with the IRS. The IRS disallowed deductions taken by the company on its tax returns for interest payments and the depreciation of assets for 1981, 1982, and 1983. WE&A sued the IRS for allowance of those deductions. In 1988, Erhard's case against the IRS was heard in Tax Court. As this book is being written, there has still not been a final decision in that case. The disputes WE&A had with the IRS were directly a result of the complex financial structure that had been established for the first two companies, the relationship of those companies and Erhard with the attorney who set them up, Harry Margolis, and the transactions surrounding the formation of WE&A.

When Erhard was first ready to offer his training and development program to the public in 1971, he didn't have the finances to start the company. Erhard was introduced to a friend's attorney, Harry Margolis. Margolis arranged to have one of his clients incorporate a business, *EST, Inc.*, and provide the needed funds for *EST, Inc.* to deliver Erhard's programs, with Margolis setting up the legal structure of the company. As a part of Margolis' deal to finance the new company, Erhard sold the rights to his programs and his technology, called the body of knowledge, to a Panamanian company, Presentaciones Musicales, S.A. (PMSA) in exchange for a one million dollar note to be paid after 10 years if the company was successful. PMSA then licensed the body of knowledge to *EST Inc.*.

Erhard said he never knew who owned IAL, the Nevada company which owned the stock of *EST, Inc.* nor was that fact determined in the Tax Court cases. "When I asked Margolis at different times over the years, he answered that it was none of my damned business,"[5] Erhard said. IAL, PMSA and other companies controlled, managed, or established by Margolis were referred to in the tax trial as Margolis system entities.

"Apparently the money coming into those earlier companies went around in a circle and wound up back in the business," Erhard said. "That all became clear when the structure that Margolis had set up was fully revealed in the *est* Tax Court case. The companies never showed much of a profit. While the revenues were very high, there were also lots of operating expenses—salaries and employee benefits, a profit-sharing retirement plan for the employees, office leases, room rentals for conducting programs, telephones, printing, travel and all the rest of the expenses every normal company has.

"Some of what was left over went to pay PMSA the licensing fees for the right to use the material I had designed and originally owned. The rest went to make interest payments to IAL on loans they made to *EST, Inc.* to purchase the assets used in operating the company."[6]

The basis for the IRS disallowing the deductions for the license fees and the interest in the *est* tax case was that the money all came back to *EST, Inc*, but along the way created the tax deductions claimed by the two original operating companies. "*EST, Inc.* made license payments to PMSA from its operating revenues," Erhard explained. "Apparently PMSA had some arrangement with IAL that allowed PMSA to transfer those funds to IAL. Subsequently, IAL made loans to *EST, Inc.* for operating expenses and the purchase of the assets they needed to keep expanding the business. In turn, *EST, Inc.* made interest payments on these loans to IAL. "The whole thing was so complicated that even the professional executives who ran the company didn't understand it completely until it all came out in the Tax Court case," Erhard said.

"From our side of the picture, it all seemed pretty simple. We were mailing checks to PMSA for the license fees. The business expanded rapidly and needed more cash to fund things like starting new programs and opening new locations that weren't immediately profitable. IAL would provide the needed cash by making loans to us. We made regular monthly interest payments on those loans to IAL. It all looked to us like damn good business planning on the part of the owners to finance the company's rapid expansion."[7]

The IRS contended, and the Tax Court confirmed, that IAL was merely loaning *EST Inc.* the money *EST Inc.* had paid to PMSA in license fees and the money *EST Inc.* paid to IAL in interest. All the money that went out of *EST Inc.* came back to *EST Inc.* in a circle. The IRS never contended that any of the money was siphoned off along the way. All the revenue *EST Inc.* received was accounted for. The revenue was reported on its tax returns and all the payments *EST Inc.* made to anyone, including the license fees and interest payments, were reported on its tax returns.

In 1974, Erhard and the executives of the company told Margolis that something needed to be done with the ownership and structure of the company. They were not only uncomfortable with the cumbersome structure of the business, but they didn't like the idea of the owners making a profit from the efforts of the hundreds of volunteers who did a lot of work in the organization. "We explained to Margolis that the success of the business was entirely predicated on customer loyalty," said Erhard. "Since the viability and growth of the company depended on the support of the participants in the programs and those who voluntarily assisted in presenting those programs, we wanted to be able to show that no corporation or individual would profit from their support.

"We told Margolis that the original owners had gotten back all the money they put into the business to get it started and had been paid hundreds of thousands of dollars in interest over the years. We were no longer willing to work for profit-making owners and wanted the ownership of the company and the body of knowledge in the hands of a charity. The owners didn't have much choice but to cooperate, they couldn't run the business without us," Erhard said.[8]

Margolis restructured the enterprise so that ownership of the stock of the new corporation, *est, a.e.c.,* was owned by an international charity, the Werner Erhard Charitable Settlement, constituted under British law. Its operation was directed by a board of directors, and it was managed by Everd van Walsum for the Alexia Trust Company, the charity's trustee.

The Werner Erhard Charitable Settlement and another charitable organization in Switzerland called the Werner Erhard Foundation for *est* together owned a holding company in Switzerland, WEF *est* Holding, AG, which in turn owned a Dutch company called Welbehagen. Welbehagen bought the body of knowledge from PMSA and licensed it to *est, a.e.c.* The part of the licensing fees that was not returned to *est, a.e.c.* by Margolis' circular money movement was used by Welbehagen's owners for their charitable projects. Erhard agreed to forgive the million dollar note PMSA owed him in exchange for PMSA's agreement to turn over the rights to charitable ownership. Erhard and the executives had accomplished part of their goals in having Margolis restructure the company to be owned by charities, but the structure was still extremely complicated and cumbersome.

Erhard said that the kind of complex tax planning used by Margolis was not uncommon and often employed by major corporations. He also said that most large companies claim some deductions which the IRS challenges. "In some cases, the company's accountants and tax experts get the IRS to see their point of view, and the IRS allows the deduction. In other cases, the company loses the argument, and the IRS disallows the deduction. If the company loses the argument, it can either pay the taxes assessed on the disallowed deduction or it can sue the IRS in Tax Court to compel the IRS to allow the deduction. At that point, the burden of proof is on the company, which has to provide enough evidence to conclusively prove that the deduction is valid under the tax code. If the company loses its case, it pays the taxes. If the company chooses to do so, it can take the case to the appellate court to attempt to get the Tax Court decision overturned. If the company wins there, the IRS pays back the taxes the company paid.

"At least some parts of this process of law are utilized by most major corporations," Erhard said. "Few major corporations have not had their turn in Tax Court. If one of these major companies loses, no one says that the deductions were illegitimate, simply that the disallowance of the deductions was upheld in Tax Court. There is a very big difference between tax evasion, which is illegal, and having reported deductions that are disallowed, which is not illegal. The IRS has never claimed any form of tax evasion against me or any company with which I've been associated."[9]

When the IRS first questioned the license and interest deductions of the earlier companies, Margolis told Erhard that the questions were routine in any audit. However, by this time, Margolis had been indicted for tax fraud in another matter, and although found not guilty, his credibility with the IRS had been tarnished. "He assured me and the executives of the company that the deductions were proper, fully documented, and that the IRS agents would ultimately allow the deductions. About a year later, when he told us that he was unable to convince the IRS or the administrative review people and he was going to take the case to Tax Court, we were still reassured. He had never lost a tax case in court."

Erhard had some business background as a Vice-President of Parents Magazine and an executive with the Grolier Society, and was familiar with the book-keeping and accounting that a field executive manages, but he had no experience in the legal and financial aspects of a large corporation. That was all handled in the home offices of the corporations where he worked. "I think it's accurate to say that I had a flair for developing people," Erhard said. "It was the secret of my success. However, I had a lot to learn about the legal and financial aspects of business. At that time, all of my personal tax returns were prepared by professional accountants. My income was large enough and my expenses were complex enough that, while I looked over the tax returns before I signed them, I can't say I always fully understood them. I trusted the professional accountants to do their job correctly. I never had any interaction with the IRS. In fact, my personal tax returns were never even audited."

Accountants in Margolis' office handled the accounting for *EST, Inc.* and sent the final financial reports of the company to the executives. Margolis' accountants also prepared and filed all the tax returns. Lawyers in his firm handled the legal aspects of setting up the first two corporations and arranged for all of the financing. The entities which owned the stock of the companies and the entities which owned the body of knowledge were also represented by Margolis. The *est* executives ran *est*, but had to leave the interaction with the other companies to Margolis.

"I had no reason to doubt Margolis' integrity and no reason to question what he was doing," Erhard said. "It is only in hindsight that anyone questioned Margolis and his methods. When we first got involved with Harry Margolis, he had an outstanding reputation. His list of clients was impressive and included well known names like Nat King Cole, jazz impresario Norman Grantz, and singer Barbara McNair who was married to Jack Rafferty. Jack was one of the people who helped to start *est* and the person who introduced me to Margolis. Jack had experience in the entertainment field and formerly had owned his own business. When we saw that we needed help in getting the business started, Jack recommended Harry Margolis."

Margolis was notably unpretentious, according to Erhard. "He was soft spoken and polite, but usually all business and usually very busy. His office, located in the small town south of San Jose called Los Gatos, was a ranch style home that had been converted into a comfortable, but unimpressive, business facility. His modest home was just behind the offices separated by a small garden. In all the time I knew him, he drove an older, medium priced automobile. He was clearly a man who had little regard for appearances.

"He seemed to know what he was doing, and was very professional in his discussions with me," Erhard said. "I later learned other things about Margolis, some of which were surprising. I learned that he was an avid socialist and had been a radical activist when he was younger. I was also told by a friend, a New York attorney, that Harry Margolis was a famous tax lawyer whose methods of tax planning were used by many of the country's best law firms."

About the same time Margolis was reforming *EST, Inc.* into *est, a.e.c.,* Erhard discovered the book *Significant Lawyers* which contained an entire chapter on Margolis. "For the first time, I really began to understand the Margolis tax planning method," Erhard said. "He said in the book that the planning methods were used for big corporations but not usually for individuals because the cost of setting up the structures involved, was more costly than the tax savings produced on the income of most individuals. I could see how the structure Margolis had set up was resulting in tax deductions, but I still had no question about their being valid because the structures used were a result of actual business transactions," Erhard said.

"I had negotiated at length with Margolis about what I would be paid to sell the rights to my material to PMSA, and I had negotiated what operational latitude we would be allowed and what financial support we would be provided by IAL, the owners of the company. I had also negotiated the terms of my employment contract. In these discussions, it was my understanding that Margolis was representing his clients, PMSA and IAL. Payments of license fees and interest are normal deductions for many corporations, and I knew that we were paying real money to PMSA for the license fees. I knew we were receiving real money when IAL made loans to us, and I knew we were paying real money when we made interest payments to IAL on those loans. I had no reason to even suspect that the transactions were in any way a sham."

When Margolis was indicted for criminal tax fraud, the *est, a.e.c.* executives were concerned and went to Erhard with a plan for protecting the company.

The plan was to hire an independent law firm in San Francisco with expertise in corporate law. "First, we wanted to know whether the deductions that were taken on the company's tax returns which were being questioned by the IRS auditing agent were legal and legitimate. We wanted to know what impact the Margolis indictment would have on the company, its directors and officers. Finally, we wanted to know what was the likelihood that Margolis was guilty of the charges against him," Erhard said. The lawyers examined the company's books and records and found nothing that appeared to be illegal regarding the challenged deductions, but could not guarantee that the case would be won in Tax Court. "They said the Tax Court's view of Margolis' methods of tax planning had dimmed and that he was no longer winning all the cases he took to Tax Court. The lawyers said that they could find no evidence that any individual had profited from the deductions and therefore the company had a better case than the ones Margolis had lost in Tax Court. They said that while Margolis' association with *est* was not well known by the public, it would hurt us in the business community. They told us that Margolis had a reputation for integrity and that they had a hard time believing he had actually done anything criminal, but of course they could not be sure. In any case, Margolis was obviously a target of the government, and anyone associated with him would also come under pressure."

Erhard and the executives reviewed the facts and discussed their options at length. They decided that in the best interests of the company, they should make arrangements to disassociate with Margolis but would wait for the outcome of his trial. Regardless of the verdict, they would then start procedures to separate the company from Margolis' complicated network. The jury found Margolis innocent in 1977, and Erhard then approached him about the new plans. "It was the first time I ever saw Margolis lose his composure," Erhard said. "I reminded him of the many times he had said that it was the lawyer's job to act in the best interest of the client. While I was sorry, it clearly was in the best interest of the client for him to disassociate with the company."

The process was not easy and took several years. Erhard retained an attorney from Coudert Brothers, a prestigious law firm with an international reputation, to head a team of lawyers and outside executives to work with *est* executives and him to design a solution to the problem. The team needed a lot of information from Margolis about the legal and financial structures. "For quite a while, Margolis was cantankerous and most uncooperative," Erhard said. "The whole process was taking way too long. I had a last meeting with Margolis in which I finally convinced him that he should cooperate with the team.

"Even with Margolis' reluctant cooperation, our team of experts still found the job dauntingly complex and difficult. Many solutions were proposed, only to find out on further research that they would not work to our satisfaction. For example, the lawyers could not find a technical method of obtaining, for the new company they were proposing, the rights to utilize the programs which I had created. I had sold the rights to PMSA in 1971 and they had been transferred to ultimate ownership by the Swiss charity in the 1975 reorganization of *est*. This critical asset was buried in the Margolis system, and extricating it was an enormous problem for the lawyers.

"Given the value of this asset as established by an independent appraisal, it would have cost more money than we felt we could raise to purchase the asset outright. Finally, they worked out a structure of leasing the rights to the material from the Swiss charity for a period of years, long enough for me to have the time to create new programs. That plan, however, was scrapped when our executives decided that they could not live with even this arms length relationship with an entity that had any association with Margolis.

"Finally, in February of 1981, I told the lawyers to establish the new business with no association with Margolis, and that we would do whatever business we could with the programs I had created after 1975 and therefore owned myself. WE&A was established with absolutely no connection whatsoever with Margolis or any Margolis controlled entity."

Erhard borrowed $15 million dollars to buy his way out of Margolis' system. The IRS contends in the WE&A tax case that the $15 million dollar loan and the transactions to buy the assets were a sham and without economic substance. The IRS disallowed deductions WE&A had claimed on its tax returns for the first three years of operation for depreciation on the assets purchased from *est, a.e.c.* and for the interest paid on the loan. "I think that the IRS had a hard time believing that the whole exercise was an effort to set ourselves up independent of Margolis," Erhard said. "Harry Margolis did not represent me personally in any way after mid-1980. Margolis never represented WE&A or participated in establishing WE&A. Of course, Margolis played a role in the transaction. How could it be otherwise? The assets needed to operate the business were owned by companies Margolis controlled and needed to be purchased from them. There was no way for me to purchase the assets without negotiating with Margolis."

Erhard explained the series of transactions that took place in 1981 to establish WE&A as an operating company. "WE&A initially received three short-term loans, one from Barclays Bank in San Francisco of $5 million dollars and two from Terla B.V. totaling slightly less than $9 million dollars. Bank records and canceled checks for the transfer of the loan proceeds totaling almost $14 million dollars from the lending institutions to WE&A were presented at the WE&A tax trial, and these payments were uncontested by the IRS.

"WE&A used the proceeds of the short term loans to pay *est, a.e.c.*, and the other Margolis controlled entities for the assets they owned such as leases and leasehold improvements on facilities around the world from which WE&A's business would be conducted, office and seminar room furniture, a computer system, telephone switching equipment, printing and copying machines, automobiles and trucks, all of which would be used by WE&A in the operation of its business. These assets were purchased at prices set by a professional independent appraisal company. WE&A's canceled checks for each of these payments and titles to the assets transferred to WE&A's name were presented in evidence and uncontested by the IRS.

Werner finally arranged long-term financing from charities interested in the work of WE&A. "The Intercultural Cooperation Foundation (ICF), a legally constituted Swiss charity that was not associated with Margolis or with any of his entities and which had no previous dealings with me or WE&A, transferred $15 million dollars from its bank accounts to the bank accounts of WE&A. This was all documented in bank records that were presented in evidence and was uncontested by the IRS. "WE&A used virtually all of the $15 million dollars it received from ICF to pay off the principal and accumulated interest on the short term loans it had received from Barclays

Bank and Terla B.V. to pay the remaining balance for the assets, and to operate the business. Every dollar of the proceeds of the $15 million dollar loan was accounted for. The canceled checks for these payments were presented in evidence and were uncontested by the IRS.

"WE&A made regular annual and then monthly interest payments over the years to ICF on the note and paid the IRS the withholding taxes due on interest payments made to foreign lenders. The canceled checks were presented in evidence and were uncontested by the IRS.

"ICF used the money it received from these payments for what the Swiss authorities who reviewed their audited records confirmed was 'consistent with its charitable purposes.'

"WE&A reported on its tax returns each of the payments made for the assets purchased with the proceeds of the loans and the payments of interest to ICF. The tax returns were prepared by Arthur Young and Company, [which later became Ernst & Young], one of the world's largest independent CPA firms, based on their certified audits of the company's books and records. All this was presented in evidence.

"The transactions involved in the loans and the various payments were all arranged or approved by recognized legal tax experts, not connected with Margolis. These experts testified that they had full knowledge of and had approved each of the transactions involved.

"The loan documents involved in the transactions were reviewed for the tax court by a Swiss lawyer who was an expert on commercial loans, by a former judge of the California appellate court, and by a former legal consultant to the U.S. Federal Reserve.

Each of these experts told the court that the loan documents were valid and enforceable under the laws of the various jurisdictions involved.

"So that I don't leave anything out of the picture, let me say that two of the multitude of assets purchased for WE&A were a sailboat which was owned by *est, a.e.c.* and works of art owned by one of the other Margolis controlled entities. However, neither of these assets was depreciated and therefore they were uncontested by the IRS. Also, with the proceeds of the loans, I paid off some personal debts I owed. Although the granting of the $15 million loan at an extremely favorable interest rate was predicated on ICF's interest in our work and on the bright prospects of the new business, WE&A was a sole proprietorship and I personally guaranteed the loans. Not one cent of the money paid to *est, a.e.c.* or to the two charities involved in the old structure ever found its way back to me or WE&A or any other entity involved in the new structure. Not one shred of evidence was presented at the WE&A tax trial to the contrary.

"In completing the picture, let me say that, as fate would have it, the special trial judge who heard the WE&A case was the very same one who had heard the *est* tax cases some years before. In the tax system, Harry Margolis had become the ultimate enemy. He'd beaten the government in jury trials, not only in the first criminal case, but in another attempt by the government to indict him only a couple of years later. The special trial judge apparently never saw that Margolis' involvement in the transactions involving WE&A was nothing more than his very reluctant cooperation in selling the assets owned by entities he controlled and that by doing so his involvement in the enterprise was brought to an end. Apparently the special trial judge thought this was another Margolis-inspired deal.

"He also took no note of the fact that I had allowed the business to be set up as a sole proprietorship in which I was personally liable, not a business form where one can hide behind the corporate veil. The special trial judge's opinion was adverse to WE&A's position on both deductions, however he denied the IRS claim of penalties for negligence in preparing the tax returns because they were prepared on advice of competent tax advisors without Margolis' involvement.

The IRS contended that WE&A paid out of its operating revenues approximately $300,000 in interest payments solely to obtain $150,000 in tax reductions. The IRS contended that the loan transactions were tax motivated and that WE&A did not really have to pay interest on the loans because the loans were not valid. If that were the case, why would WE&A pay $300,000 out to realize a reduction in taxes of only $150,000? This suggests that the payment of the interest was not done for the purpose of reducing its taxes, but rather because it was a valid debt. Clearly, it cost WE&A significantly more in interest payments than the reduction in taxes allowed by the tax code on interest payments. Interest paid on the $15 million dollar loan from 1981 to 1988 totaled $2 million and deduction of that interest amounted to a reduction of $1 million in taxes and the only reason WE&A paid $2 million in interest was because it had a valid obligation to ICF upon which interest was due, not to reduce taxes. Moreover, the $1 million of principal that was paid back to ICF on the part of the loan covered by a demand note was paid solely because there was a valid obligation to do so, not to reduce taxes since such payment resulted in no deduction and therefore in no reduction of taxes.[10]

"Senior Tax Court judge, Irene Scott, accepted WE&A's request for consideration and at the moment the outcome of the trial is awaiting her final decision. I am confident she will provide some relief from the special trial judge's opinion, and I fully expect that all the deductions will be completely upheld on appeal."

There have been reports over the years that Erhard has secret Swiss bank accounts or money stashed away somewhere, rumors he said are simply false. "There are probably not many people in the world whose personal and business finances have been more carefully scrutinized and investigated than my own," he said. "I guess something easily in excess of a couple of million dollars has been spent by opposing attorneys and government investigators minutely examining my financial life. The money was wasted because there are no hidden assets, there is no pot of gold. Perhaps even more telling is the fact that in the WE&A tax case, a former IRS expert on what is called source and application, testified that he had conducted a thorough investigation of my personal and business finances. He told the court that he was able to account for every dollar of business revenue and personal income I had access to from the beginning of *EST* through May 31, 1981," said Erhard.[11]

It was not the IRS contending that there were any secret or unreported funds somewhere. That agency knew where all the money came from and where all the money went. It's been other people accusing Erhard of hiding money, those who are committed to doing damage to him, including his ex-wife, Ellen Erhard.

I was told by Art Schreiber, the general counsel and one of the senior executives of WE&A, that the lack of cash reserves needed to support the operations of WE&A from time to time in the late 1980s was in large part attributable to the multi-million dollar cost of Ellen Erhard's divorce case. Under California family law, Erhard was required to pay not only his own attorneys' fees, but all his wife's attorneys' fees and costs. "It appears that cash that should have been used to support the business was instead used up in Ellen's case," Schreiber said.[12]

Journalists reporting on Erhard's transactions in establishing WE&A and on the various phases of the tax court proceedings have implied, if not said outright, that he paid the $15 million dollars to himself, which is completely disproved by the court records. In June 1981 WE&A borrowed, with the help of Margolis, because it had no banking credibility of its own yet, $5 million from Barclays Bank of California at 19 7/8 percent interest rate. The $287,169 in interest paid to Barclays for this loan was allowed by the IRS. WE&A borrowed an additional $2.2 million from Terla B.V. in June 1981 and another $6,580,000 in August 1981 at 20 percent interest rate. IRS did not allow the deduction for the $196,285 paid in interest to Terla on these loans.

The combined $13,780,000 borrowed in the summer of 1981 was used for the following: $865,000 to Werner Erhard Charitable Settlement for the art work in the various centers and properties; $1,062,847 to Barclays Bank in the Netherlands to terminate a loan Margolis had arranged for Erhard earlier; $250,000 to Associated Advisors, a Margolis system entity, to repay a loan; $229,000 to Associated Advisors, for purchase of the sailboat Sirona; $342,829 to Antigua Banking Limited to repay a loan; $94,449 to Antigua to purchase loans of *est* employees who were to become WE&A employees; $6,400,660 to *est, a.e.c.* for operating assets (of which $4,876,277 was claimed as depreciable and subsequently disallowed by the IRS); $50,000 to PMSA for a quit-claim deed to the body of knowledge; $1,385,000 to Welbehagen for the body of knowledge, which was not depreciated by WE&A; and $3,099,323 for WE&A operating capital— utilities, telephone, salaries, etc.

The long-term $14 million loan from ICF in September 1981 with 2 percent interest rate was used to repay Barclays and Terla the $13,780,000 short-term loans plus the interest of $35,972 to Barclays (an earlier interest payment of $251,197 had been paid from WE&A's operating funds) and $196,285 to Terla—a total of $14,012,257. In November Erhard paid an additional $1,547,645 to *est, a.e.c.* for adjusted sales prices of the assets. He borrowed another $1 million from ICF at 2 percent interest rate payable on demand. This $1 million was repaid in November 1985. The records show that none of the payments made by WE&A to disentangle from the Margolis system ever came back to Erhard or to WE&A.[13] Although the principal of the $14 million loan was due in September 1991, most of that loan remains outstanding.

In the midst of the negative media blitz about Erhard, he decided the best thing to do to preserve the technology he had developed, and thereby allow the programs to continue to be made available in the future, was to remove himself from it. After a few weeks of negotiations, in February 1991, he sold WE&A to the employees who formed a new company and named it Landmark Education Corporation. That action also got a lot of attention from the press as did everything else Erhard did.

The IRS was being kept abreast of the press's coverage of Erhard and was also being kept informed of his activities by Paul Gutfreund and Randy Loftin, both of whom were involved in lawsuits pending against Erhard. According to a memo written to the Sacramento District IRS office, Revenue Officer Greg Gillen and Revenue Agent Lou Kraushaar used information provided by Gutfreund and Loftin and contacted several other people trying to determine if Erhard was hiding or transferring assets to avoid the tax liability that was expected to be assessed by the Tax Court.[14]

Erhard was, in fact, liquidating his assets, but not for the reasons Gutfreund and Loftin assumed and subsequently convinced Gillen and Kraushaar was happening. When he sold the WE&A assets to the former employees, Erhard kept most of the liabilities of the company including the outstanding $14 million dollar obligation to ICF, on which only interest payments had been made up to then. The money Erhard received from his assets was going directly to pay off the WE&A creditors that were still on the books when WE&A was sold. The down payment he received from the employees for the company was applied to the $14 million dollar loan. The boat Erhard lived on was owned by Gary Grace and leased by Erhard, so he received no money from its sale.[15]

However, instead of talking directly with Erhard or any of the people involved with his actions, the IRS agents relied on information from Gutfreund, Loftin, and other Erhard foes like Vincent Drucker. The IRS agents also used newspaper accounts that Erhard had sold his business and fled the country to determine that he was trying to evade his tax liability which, in fact, was not even a liability yet since Judge Scott had not issued a final opinion in the matter. The agents said they didn't talk to Erhard or his close associates because they didn't want to alert him of their investigation.[16]

In April 1991, the IRS took an unprecedented action against Erhard by filing a jeopardy assessment against him, thereby placing liens on the proceeds of property he had sold and property that he was in the process of selling. Erhard brought a lawsuit against the IRS in the U.S. District Court in San Francisco to set aside the jeopardy assessment saying that until a tax is actually determined to be due, the action was illegal. By the time the hearing for that case came up, the tax special trial judge, James M. Gussis, had just issued an opinion, which still had to go to the full Tax Court judge for review. Although a final judgment had not been made, the IRS viewed it as one, and left the jeopardy assessment in place.

Contrary to what was generally reported in the press about Erhard and his businesses over the years, he said he was never a millionaire, never milked the company or sequestered funds. Gary Grace, who was chief financial officer of *est, a.e.c.* for four years in the late 1970s, managed Erhard's personal finances from June 1980 until Erhard left in 1991. Grace said it was true that although Erhard lived well, he was not a millionaire, and he didn't have money stashed away anywhere. "There were times during those 11 years that Werner had some money, maybe several hundred thousand dollars," Grace said. "But even if he had a million dollars, he still owed the $14 million and you can't be a millionaire when your liabilities are more than your assets. What money he did get always went back into the company."

Grace explained that while Erhard did not have or accumulate wealth, he "experienced" wealth, a distinction that Erhard spoke about in the early years of the business when he was accused of extravagance with the employees. "He wanted to take particularly good care of the staff with benefits and experiences," Grace said.

"He would close down the business at the end of each year and take everyone on a vacation—a completely paid for vacation. They'd go to Hawaii or Mexico, they went on a cruise. Everyone lived it up, in a style they weren't accustomed to. They experienced wealth." Grace said that practice stopped after the first few years when the staff grew to incorporate so many people.

"Werner did, in fact, live very well and many people would probably think he had the lifestyle of a millionaire. But he worked very long hours and very hard, and he appreciated the benefits of nice accommodations and transportation, fine wines, cigars. Yet, he really didn't have the kind of wealth portrayed in the media."[15]

Erhard was also asked about his "lavish" lifestyle and rumors of his squandering money. "Much of what has been reported about my lifestyle is either outright false or reported on in an entirely misleading way. On the other hand, I am guilty to some degree. I have lived well, and in some instances lavishly, and I suppose that I have even squandered money at times. But there is more to the story than that.

"From time to time, some of the company executives complained about the facilities the company provided for me, and the business expenses I incurred, but not one of the people who worked closely with me on a day to day basis ever had a problem with the way I lived. For the most part, I worked 15 to 20 hours a day. And for the most part, I worked seven days a week. Without what I produced the company could not have existed. I don't think that it is an overstatement to say that

I was indispensable to the success of the company.

"I had been very well paid by the two major corporations I worked for before *EST, Inc.* and had
lived well for quite a long time. At the beginning of
EST, Inc., my salary was modest, my facilities spar-
tan, and my expenses kept to a minimum. As the
revenues of the company expanded, and did so at
a remarkable rate, I was provided with better and
better facilities. There were bonuses, and my salary
kept growing. I have no apologies for my lifestyle.
I did not make money, I earned it. In gratitude for
the opportunities I had in life, I tried to give something back, not only through the work I did, but
through various charitable endeavors."[18]

The public, however, did not have the opportunity during the media firestorm of negative allegations that destroyed Erhard to find out what he was
really like and make its own decisions about him.
Real journalism was missing. The press denied the
public the full story, especially the part of the story
that would have made the allegations about Erhard
unbelievable. The contributions he had made to society and the difference he had made in so many
people's lives were never mentioned.

[1] Seth Rosenfeld, "Erhard owes $5.5 million, tax court says," *San Fran
cisco Examiner*, July 31, 1991, p. A-6; "IRS Accuses *est* Head of Tax
Dodging," *Los Angeles Times*, August 1, 1991; Rex Bossert, "IRS Says
Personal Growth Guru Is Mastermind of Money Shams," *San Francisco
Daily Journal*, July 31, 1991; Don Lattin, "More Legal Woes for Erhard:
New suit says sale of *est* founder's seminar business was fraudulent,"
The San Francisco Chronicle, March 26, 1991; Martha Groves, "Guru
Erhard Accused of Trying To Hide Assets," *Los Angeles Times*, March
27, 1991; Elizabeth Fernandez,"IRS puts lien on Erhard's assets," *San
Francisco Examiner*, April 12, 1991; "IRS: *EST* founder avoided taxes,"
Associated Press, August 2, 1991.

[2] Interviews with Werner Erhard, September 15, 1991; Art Schreiber,
December 31, 1991; Rik Super, May 31, 1992; Gary Grace, June 4, 1992;
Mike Saltzman, July 1, 1992.

[3] Werner H. Erhard and Ellen V. Erhard v. Commissioner of Internal Revenue, U.S. Tax Court, Brief for Petitioner, p. 35.

[4] Interview with Werner Erhard, September 15, 1991.

[5] Interview with Werner Erhard, September 15, 1991.

[6] Interview with Werner Erhard, September 15, 1991.

[7] Interview with Werner Erhard, September 15, 1991.

[8] Interview with Werner Erhard, September 15, 1991.

[9] Interview with Werner Erhard, September 15, 1991.

[10] Erhard v. IRS, Motion for Reconsideration, p. 69.

[11] Interview with Werner Erhard, September 15, 1991; Erhard v.IRS, Brief for Petitioner, p. 39.

[12] Interview with Art Schreiber, July 9, 1992.

[13] Erhard v. IRS, Brief for Petitioner, p. 70-91.

[14] IRS Memorandum to Sacramento District Counsel from Greg Gillen and Lou Kraushaar, March 27, 1991. Exhibit from the Jeopardy Assessment trial.

[15] Interviews with Gary Grace, June 4, 1992 and Rik Super, May 31,1992.

[16] IRS Memorandum, March 27, 1991.

[17] Interview with Gary Grace, June 4, 1992.

[18] Interview with Werner Erhard, September 15, 1991.

CHAPTER IX
MAKING A DIFFERENCE

When most people talk about transformation, they mean the act of changing the appearance, nature, or function of something—the classic dictionary definition. A caterpillar transforms into a butterfly; water transforms into ice. When Werner Erhard's programs are referred to as transformational, it means altering the context in which things occur for people, for institutions, and for society as a whole. When the context for something alters, things are viewed differently and new possibilities one didn't previously see are revealed. Predispositions and prejudices are seen for what they are, giving people the freedom to create anew their values, beliefs, and interpretations of life.

For example, Alan Menken, the New York composer who won four Academy awards for his musical scores in "The Little Mermaid" and "Beauty and the Beast" said that he gave up some of his prejudices after participating in Erhard's courses. "I used to think I was responsible for only my part of a project. I realized I'm really responsible for the success of the entire project," Menken said. "That kind of work is a very powerful tool for fulfilling goals and realizing my intentions."[1] Erhard has always been committed to making that kind of difference, not just for individuals, but for the environments in which they live and operate.

By the time Erhard sold his company, Werner Erhard and Associates, and went into self-imposed exile in February 1991, over one million people had participated in the programs he designed, none of which he ever advertised. People found out about his work from friends, spouses, relatives, or co-workers who had participated and found value in their participation. Erhard intended for it to be that way. He wasn't interested in wasting people's time or money. He was interested in providing opportunities for people to make a difference in their lives, their communities and the world.

"If a program makes a difference for people, they tend to want to share that with others. That's the way I've built everything I've ever built—on the results for people I've worked with," Erhard said.[2]

Participants in Erhard's courses come from all strata of society, ranging from students and housewives to heads of corporations and elected government officials, and include well-known celebrities such as John Denver, Valerie Harper, Yoko Ono, Carly Simon, gold medalist John Curry, author Ken Blanchard, Joanne Woodward, Polly Bergen, Diana Ross and hundreds of others.

Actor Raul Julia, recently of "The Addams Family" fame, started participating in Erhard's programs in 1974. Over the next two years, Julia and Erhard had become close. In 1976, Erhard was sponsoring a trip

to the United States of Swami Baba Muktananda of
India and had made arrangements for Muktananda
to perform a wedding ceremony for Julia and his
wife, Merel. "I heard that Werner was going back
to India with Baba and asked him if I could go with
them," Julia said in a telephone interview from New
York where he was wrapping up his starring role
in "The Man of La Mancha" on Broadway. "He told
me his only concern was that I would disrupt the
momentum of my successful acting career. I said it
would be worth it." Julia and his wife accompanied
Erhard and Muktananda to India where they spent
a month together.[3]

As Julia's acting career developed over the years,
he always acknowledged Erhard and his work as
having made a huge difference in his life, and in fact,
continued to participate in Erhard's work through
out the years when time allowed. "I've talked about
my relationship with Werner to reporters and never
gotten any flak. They've faithfully printed what I
said accurately and never said anything negative,"
said Julia. That is until the *National Enquirer* published a story in January 1992 saying Julia was
"obsessed with a cult leader (Erhard) accused of beatings and sexual abuse."[4] Even then Julia wasn't
deterred from speaking out in support of his friend.
He said he recently was on the "Dick Cavett" show
and talked about Erhard. "I told him (Cavett) I didn't
believe the *60 Minutes* show and that eventually that
whole mess was going to get cleared up. He just
laughed and moved on to the next subject."[5]

The core programs of the work Erhard developed,
the *est* Training up to 1984 and the Forum after
1985, were based on his original theories and models
of thinking. The Forum is a rigorous inquiry into
what shapes human beings. The Forum allows people to have a profound understanding of themselves

by coming to grips with fundamental issues of being human and resolving those issues, in a way that allows them to generate new possibilities beyond what had previously been available. Done in a group, participants can see themselves in others, and the group dynamic also accelerates the process dramatically. People in the Forum examine decisions, experiences, and situations that have shaped their lives. Participants see the depth that they are shaped by past events and experiences, but in a way that they can step outside of past patterns of behavior. Possibilities and freedoms previously obscured and unavailable are revealed. The people who lead the course are highly trained and present the programs in a provocative, intentional, and respectful manner.[6]

Those who enrolled in the *est* Training and the Forum generally were well-educated and successful in both their personal lives and professions. Studies, questionnaires, surveys, and personal conversations have shown that participants in Erhard's programs received a wide range of benefits from their participation. The most recent study of the Forum, which replaced the *est* Training in 1985, was conducted in the late 1980s by Daniel Yankelovich, author of *New Rules: Searching for Self-Fulfillment in a World Turned Upside Down* and owner of one of the most prestigious public opinion analysis firms.

According to Yankelovich, "Several of the study's findings surprised me quite a bit, especially the large number of participants for whom the Forum proved to be 'one of the most valued experiences of my life.' This is not a sentiment that people, particularly successful, well-educated people, express lightly.

"More than seven out of ten participants found the Forum to be one of their most rewarding experiences. To me, this suggests that the Forum addresses many of people's most profound concerns; how to improve their personal relationships, how to be a more effective person, how to think productively about their lives and goals."[7]

Ninety-five percent of the 1,370 participants from 18 Forums whom Yankelovich surveyed said that the Forum had specific, practical value for many aspects of their lives. Ninety-three percent said it was well worth their time and effort and that it better prepared them for situations and challenges that may arise in the future.

The major benefits people reported in the Yankelovich study included: a better understanding of all kinds of relationships, more motivation and commitment, improved communication with others, a better understanding of their abilities and limitations, more productivity apart from the job, the ability to be closer and more intimate with people, a clearer sense of direction, and help in setting life's priorities.

Nancy Hogshead, a swimmer who won three gold medals in the 1984 Olympics, took the Forum in 1986, followed by several other programs offered by WE&A. She said her relationship with her younger sister, who also had taken the Forum, improved tremendously after their participation. "I was frequently mad at her because she was a spoiled brat and didn't have to work as hard as I did," Hogshead said. "And my sister was mad at me because she had to have this famous swimmer sister who set the standard so high." That's all changed according to Hogshead, who is now 30 and a motivational speaker and teacher. "We have so much fun now and to think we could have missed out on all that. She is so funny and so witty."[8]

Hogshead said she views her continuing participation in the programs Erhard created as valuable training for her current career. (She retired from competitive swimming after the 1984 Olympics.) "It keeps me in touch with what excites me about my job and my life," she said. "And when I catch myself thinking 'I'm not good enough,' or 'I'm not tough enough,' I know it isn't true. I can laugh at myself for thinking it."

Ted Danson, star of the television series "Cheers" and the hit movies "Three Men and a Baby" and "Three Men and a Little Lady," told *Parade Magazine* in a February 1991 interview that his life turned around after taking the Training in 1976. "What I walked away with," he said, "was that, for the first time, I felt 'this is my movie,' I could affect the way I wanted my life to go. It's a cliche by now, but you do 'create your own reality.' People don't do it to you." He met Cassandra Coates in one of Erhard's programs, and six months later, she became his second wife. They are still together today out of the commitment they were able to make to each other from the very beginning.[9]

While, as a result of their participation in the *est* Training or the Forum, many people reported being able to enhance their close, and sometimes estranged, relationships, especially with parents or other family members. They also usually found that without trying, they were more motivated to accomplish things that were important to them. They found that committing themselves to do something was much more powerful than wishing or hoping things were a certain way.

A Columbia University professor of real estate development and urban planning, Marc Weiss, said that Erhard's courses had a huge impact on his work in the community. He realized that he could do something about the political and social issues that were important to him. "I made it a central commitment of my life for everyone in America to be well-housed," Weiss said. "This work helped me be more willing to take that on, and that commitment is part of my life now in everything I do, speaking, writing, teaching, and consulting."[10]

Dick D'Amato found that his participation in the *est* Training in the early 1980s, the only Erhard course he ever took, made a big difference in the way he relates with people, which he thinks is particularly important in the political arena. As the Aide to the Senate Appropriations Committee in Washington, D.C., D'Amato spends a lot of time with constituents of varying interests. "I relate to people in a more open way. I avoid drawing lines on issues and I am able to bring about consensus a lot more easily," D'Amato said. "I can see the pros and cons of issues more clearly." On a more personal level, he said the *est* Training had also helped him avoid compartmentalizing his personal relationships.[11]

Paul Dietrich was a Missouri state legislator and publisher of *Saturday Review Magazine* when he first took the Training in the 1970s. Dietrich is now the U.S. counsel of record for the Republic of Georgia and general counsel for the Gorbachev Foundation in the U.S. One of the things Dietrich said most impressed him was Erhard's ability to translate material of the great philosophers and make their thinking available to average people. "In that, I think Werner was a genius," Dietrich said. "You've got to give the guy enormous credit. Werner took their ideas and was able to apply them in the world."[12]

Erhard's work had an impact in other arenas, going beyond the individuals—and families or associates of individuals—who participated in his work.

Several independent non-profit organizations were established during the 1970s and 1980s as a direct result of people with broad interests and commitments participating in his programs. Prison Possibilities, the Mastery Foundation, the Hunger Project, the Education Network, and the Breakthrough Foundation are a few of those.

When Eugene Featherstone took the Forum in the mid-1980s, he said he had been hiding the fact that he was an ex-convict, having served three years in prison for dealing drugs and bank robbery. "I was out of prison, but still a prisoner," he said.[13] During the Forum, Featherstone decided to take a chance and share his past. "I felt like 500 pounds dropped from my shoulders when I stood up and told the truth." He said he saw that what could be realized from the Forum would be an invaluable resource for prisoners, a way that they could start to take responsibility for themselves, and he proceeded to put his ideas into action.

Featherstone found others who were interested in the same thing. Peggy LaMarre, a former prison therapist, was one. They joined forces, established Prison Possibilities, and convinced some Michigan prison officials to allow the Forum to be delivered to the prisoners. Although the inmates didn't have to pay for taking the Forum, they were required to relinquish visiting privileges in exchange for their enrollment to give them a degree of investment in the program. The results after three Forums conducted in the prisons were phenomenal. Incidents of misconduct among the prisoners who participated dropped 44% and participation in other rehabilitation programs and voluntary work assignments increased dramatically—78%. The prisoners also reported personal successes such as reuniting with their families, finding and keeping jobs, and resuming their education. After his participation in the Forum, a felon previously convicted of kidnap and robbery told a newspaper reporter "I used to blame other people for my shortcomings. Now I have a new beginning in life, one that allows me to use my talent, skill and intelligence, instead of my mask and gun. One that will allow me to love instead of hate."

Featherstone said that Prison Possibilities is active in other states—Colorado, Delaware, and parts of California, with more states in the works—and he's ready to move on to other things now that he's seen what he's capable of accomplishing. "I see the impact that my life has on the world and other people. I take more risks to contribute in places where I would play safe and let somebody else do it in the past," Featherstone said, pointing out that he had grown up in Arkansas, picking cotton and working in factories. As a black youth in the South, he didn't think he had a future. And that's where his next project is taking him—working with young gang members before they become part of the prison system.

Dan Miller started working with troubled youth in the late 1970s. He worked with the Foreign Service in India and with an urban development corporation in New York before he got involved with Erhard's work. Miller said he had noticed that despite the value of the institutions and programs with which he had been involved and how much they accomplished, one thing was missing. "The people being helped were not empowered to take charge of their own lives," Miller said.[14] Miller took the *est* Training in 1976 and volunteered his services at Erhard events in New York. When he met Erhard in 1978, Miller asked whether Erhard thought his work could be applied to deal with social and urban issues and provide the empowerment Miller had discovered was missing. Erhard said yes and offered to volunteer his time, use of his programs, and a support network at no cost to Miller if he really wanted to do something.

Miller took Erhard seriously. In late 1978, he moved to San Francisco for easier access to Erhard and established the non-profit Breakthrough Foundation. "Werner kept his word," Miller said. "He never had a formal role with the organization. We never paid him. He was never on the board or anything. He did volunteer his time, leading large community workshops in the early 1980s; he helped develop our original program; and he provided a network of support for our work."

Youth at Risk started out as one of many projects of the Breakthrough Foundation but eventually became the organization's primary program. According to Miller, by the time he left the organization at the end of 1991, close to 30 programs had been set up in 19 separate communities to work with youth in trouble. Miller said that several studies have confirmed the positive results he could see on his own. "For the hard-core kids we worked with, there was a 50% drop in recidivism of felony crimes; one-third drop in use of drugs; 75% decrease in truancy; and an increase in the number of hours worked during a week." He said he really knew the program was making a difference when "they started looking beyond themselves and started contributing back to the community."

Miller said a side benefit he observed was in the thousands of volunteers working with their programs. "People who never before saw a way to actually do something in their communities, certainly in this arena, found that they could do something and make a difference."

Thousands of participants in various Erhard semi-

nars have also volunteered time "assisting" and
working to put on programs for others. The volunteer aspect of Erhard's work is unique in that the
value for those who have taken on some project
around the seminars and programs seems to out-
weigh what those volunteers put into the programs
of their time and work.

While professor of theater at the University of
Wisconsin in Milwaukee, Sandy Robbins, was
encouraged by another professor to take the *est*
Training. "It sounded like pop psychology to me,"
Robbins said.[15] However, because he had great
respect for the other professor, Robbins signed up
in 1980. "It was the most profound and valuable
educational program I've ever taken," Robbins said.
"I subsequently recommended it to all my colleagues
and students. Even though it was controversial, it
was well worth the heat for the value produced."
Robbins, who currently chairs the Department of
Theater at the University of Delaware where he
encourages both staff and students to participate in
the courses Erhard designed, said that he could see
the programs making a significant difference in the
creativity of his students.

Because of Robbins' credentials as an educator, he
was asked in 1985 to serve on the board of the Education Network, an independent non-profit organization which was established in 1983 by a group of
educators who had participated in Erhard's programs. The purpose of the organization was to bring
together students, teachers, parents, and public officials who are committed to increasing school atten-
dance and reducing drop-out rates as well as
improving the quality of education. Erhard was not
officially associated with the Education Network, but
he occasionally led courses for the Network and consulted with the board of directors upon request.

The same year the Education Network was founded, a group of religious leaders also discovered Erhard's work and formed their own non-profit organization, the Mastery Foundation, which was designed to empower those who minister. The Reverend Basil Pennington, a Roman Catholic priest and Cisterian monk in Massachusetts, said that he first met Erhard at an event about hunger in Boston. Pennington had already heard of Erhard from a doctoral student at Massachusetts Institute of Technology who had told Pennington how she returned to the church as a result of the *est* Training. Pennington was very interested in finding out more about Erhard and his work.

"I began thinking maybe there was something there that we could capture for the clergy—some of that same transforming experience," Pennington said.[16] He soon found others—bishops, priests, ministers, and rabbis—who were thinking along the same lines. "We got together, formed a board, and asked Werner to help design a course to empower the clergy in their ministry," Pennington said. "We called the course 'Making a Difference: A Course for Those Who Minister' and created the Mastery Foundation."

A Catholic priest from San Francisco, Gerry O'Rourke, was one of the clergy members working with Pennington to set up the Mastery Foundation. O'Rourke, who was ordained in 1950, was seriously considering leaving the priesthood when he took the *est* Training in 1973. After a few years, O'Rourke decided to return to the church. "I learned the power of distinctions from his work (Erhard's courses), and that's a lot of what theology is, distinctions. This was very empowering for me and enhanced my love of God and my ability for forgiveness," O'Rourke said.[17]

Perhaps one of the most far-reaching impacts of Erhard's work has been in the area of hunger. Concerned that an estimated one billion people in the world live in poverty and face hunger on a daily basis, Erhard, John Denver, and Robert Fuller founded The Hunger Project in 1977 to address the public indifference, ignorance, and resignation regarding chronic hunger. The purpose of The Hunger Project was to create a worldwide movement to end hunger in the world by the year 2000.

According to Ted Howard, former director of communications and global chief operating officer for The Hunger Project, what was lacking to bring about the end of death by starvation was not the technological know how or resources, but rather the will and commitment of both developed and Third World nations. "The critical ingredient was the involvement of people who could create that global momentum to make the ending of hunger a priority," Howard said. "The Hunger Project focused on reaching individual men, women, and children to generate with them that commitment. The thrust of the program was basically communication, information, education and enrollment of people to take the action in their own lives to help generate this commitment."

Although the organization was not designed to feed hungry people, Howard said that "as an expression of the organization's support of that kind of work, it gave several million dollars in grants to organizations that provided food and relief to the hungry. The Hunger Project didn't move in that arena because there were other organizations far better equipped to do that. The piece that we could add to that was this commitment of individuals around the world. We asked people to look into their own lives for what they could do to make a difference.

We didn't direct them, we asked them to think for themselves. A lot of people raised money not only for the Hunger Project but for other organizations addressing hunger as well. They did a lot of public-awareness, consciousness-raising things; they put up billboards in their communities, and wrote articles. People got involved in letter-writing campaigns to Congress. A group in Hollywood had celebrities go on talk shows to talk about hunger. People went to work for local hunger organizations and food banks. People wrote books, musicians wrote songs, artists created posters."[18]

The Hunger Project now has more than 6 million people who carry out its work with organized activities in 37 countries. The organization is on the roster of the Economic and Social Council of the United Nations and is a member of the American Council for Voluntary International Action.

The Hunger Project has been characterized as a "strategic organization"—one which acts to create a new future beyond the framework of existing problems and opportunities. James Grant, executive director of UNICEF, said that "The Hunger Project demonstrates powerfully that humankind has the knowledge and means to eliminate widespread hunger within our lifetime."[19] President George Bush said "People who are hungry . . . need more than contributions of food. With the innovative ideas and devoted work of people such as Hunger Project volunteers, we can spread the light of hope to people in need."[20]

Erhard established the Werner Erhard Foundation in 1973 to "forward, nurture and fund projects that open new possibilities for human thinking, growth and achievement, and that better the human condition through non-profit voluntary action."[21] From the time it was created until it recently closed, the

Foundation granted more than $3 million for over
300 projects that critically impacted the quality of
people's lives. Some examples of the kinds of
projects supported included emergency relief for
victims of the earthquake that crippled Armenia in
the late 1980s, assistance to private voluntary organizations working to relieve the effects of famine in
the Sudan, assistance in the clean-up efforts after the
Alaskan oil spill, aid to people of Bangladesh in the
wake of flooding that devastated the region, grants
to national organizations engaged in AIDS research,
a national conference on voluntarism, and grants to
individuals engaged in leading-edge work in the
sciences, humanities, and the arts.

The Foundation also funded two major ongoing
projects. From his commitment to create a "world
that works for everyone," Erhard was extremely
interested in East-West relations. As a result, the
US/USSR Project was designed in 1979 as an educational exchange to make the principles of communication, management, and creative thinking available to the people of the Soviet Union. Erhard met
with Valentin Bereskov, a Soviet embassy official,
in 1980 to start the discussion. After lengthy negotiations and two auditions before Soviet officials,
Erhard was invited in 1986 by the Soviet government
to conduct a course in Moscow for executives,
managers and scholars under the auspices of the
Znaniye (All Union Knowledge) Society, the prime
vehicle for adult education in the Soviet Union at
the time.[22] Although Erhard is now in exile from the
United States and the Foundation has closed, he con-
tinues his consulting work with Soviet leaders.

The second major project funded by the Foundation was the Ethiopia Project. Erhard was one of the
first individuals who expressed interest in assisting
the five to seven million people of Ethiopia who

were threatened by the severe drought of 1987 while also embroiled in a devastating civil war. Erhard went to the country to see first-hand the situation and determine what actions Americans could take that would have the greatest impact. After his trip, Erhard launched a nationwide campaign to inform the public of the suffering of the Ethiopian people and the threat they faced of massive starvation. Tens of thousands of action packets were sent out. Over half of those reached by Erhard's mailing reported that they had donated money to independent relief efforts or taken some other action to support it.[23]

In 1988, Erhard received the Mahatma Gandhi Humanitarian Award for his leadership in addressing such broad-based social concerns. This award was bestowed on Erhard by the Gandhi Memorial International Foundation, an organization founded by Gandhi's grand-nephew, Yogesh Gandhi, to continue Gandhi's teachings of non-violence.[24]

"The thing that really got me about the *60 Minutes* attack on Werner was the incredible stupidity of the assault," said Mark Kamin. "Werner will be fine no matter what happens. Who pays the price for a sensational piece of trashy journalism are all those thousands of people who used Erhard's stand to empower themselves and others to make a difference. They tried to silence a real champion for the dignity of human beings. It's incredible."[25]

[1] Interview with Alan Menken, June 19, 1992

[2] Interview with Werner Erhard, September 15, 1991.

[3] Interview with Raul Julia, June 24, 1992.

[4] Jeffrey Rodack and David Duffy, "'Addams Family' star obsessed with a cult leader accused of beatings & sexual abuse," *National Enquirer*, January 21, 1992.

[5] Interview with Raul Julia, June 24, 192.

[6] Summary by Harry Rosenberg, July 6, 1992.

[7] From Forum brochure, 1991.

[8] Interview with Nancy Hogshead, June 18, 1992.

[9] Claire Carter, "How a 'Sweet-But Shallow' Guy Grew Up," *Parade,* February 10, 1991.

[10] Interview with Marc Weiss, June 1, 1992

[11] Interview with Dick D'Amato, June 4, 1992.

[12] Interview with Paul Dietrich, June 8, 1992.

[13] Interview with Eugene Featherstone, May 28, 1992.

[14] Interview with Dan Miller, June 18, 1992.

[15] Interview with Sandy Robbins, June 2, 1992.

[16] Interview with Father Basil Pennington, June 1, 1992.

[17] Interview with Father Gerry O'Rourke, May 24, 1992.

[18] Interview with Ted Howard, June 6, 1992.

[19] Hunger Project brochure.

[20] Hunger Project brochure.

[21] Werner Erhard Foundation brochure and literature.

[22] Robert S. Greenberger, "The Soviets Discover Werner Erhard," *The Wall Street Journal,* December 3, 1986; background materials from the Werner Erhard Foundation.

[23] Werner Erhard, "Fighting hunger: We learn from success, too," editorial in the *Chicago Tribune,* November 21, 1988; background material from Werner Erhard & Associates.

[24] "International Humanitarian Award Goes To You," *The Review*, newsletter published by Werner Erhard & Associates, January 1989, p. 9.

[25] Interview with Mark Kamin, June 7, 1992.

CHAPTER X
THE TALL POPPY

By all accounts, Erhard is an extraordinary man—virtually everyone who came in contact with him knew that, even those who became his enemies. Throughout the years some of the people who were around him revered him almost to omnipotence, they thought he could do no wrong.

Mark Kamin, who has known Erhard since the beginnings of *est* and has remained close to him over the years, said that Erhard didn't like or encourage people to think of him that way. "The people in *est* and to, a lesser degree, Werner Erhard and Associates, used to create an image of Werner as perfect," Kamin said. "They built him up to be a demigod, a model. Leaders in the organization would sometimes say 'How would Werner do it?' or 'That's not the way Werner would do it.' Now, Werner trusted others to run those companies. I sensed there were times he would get furious when he found out that someone who worked for him had said this or

that 'should be the same way Werner would do it.'
He was not excited about that stuff. Werner is no
demigod. He provides an opportunity for people to
be responsible for their lives.''[1]

Kamin thinks that people who viewed Erhard as
a demigod also became his biggest critics when he
did something inconsistent with how they thought
he should be. It called into question everything about
him, everything that he stood for—it made him suspect in their eyes. ''I think that's a lot of what happened with some of the people who were close to
him,'' Kamin said. He gave an example of a phone
conversation he had a few days after the *60 Minutes*
show that was supposed to be with Erhard and
another associate. Erhard, who was already in exile
out of the country, didn't make it for the call. ''The
other person said 'Well, what happened to Mr.
Responsibility, the guy who teaches everybody how
to keep their word?' This associate was really angry.
Now, I happen to know the person who made the
critical comment wasn't perfect. However, it became
a big deal that Werner wasn't on the call. Werner
later apologized to me and this guy. His car had broken down and he didn't have a way to get to a phone
at the appointed time. But the bottom line is that
the expectations around Werner are enormous—if
he screws up, it's magnified times a hundred.''[2]

When Kamin first noticed how Erhard lived and
worked, he had the same problem dealing with
Erhard's imperfections. ''For example, Werner
smokes; he works two or three days at a time without sleeping—relentless work; he doesn't exercise,''
Kamin said. ''I don't smoke, I exercise, I eat healthy
foods. To me, one should be that way. When I found
out Werner wasn't that way, I thought maybe he's
a fraud, maybe he's not valid. Then I realized that
doesn't really mean anything. He never agreed not

to smoke cigarettes and not to drink coffee. He never agreed to exercise. That doesn't have anything to do with what I've gotten out of this work or who the guy is and what he contributes."[3]

Kamin also thinks that Erhard was a man before his time—that the world just wasn't ready for him and his ideas. He was unique, he operated differently than most people, and he was totally committed to his work and to providing opportunities for people to be great. He didn't fit the paradigm of the era— people's way of perceiving and explaining their environment.

"It was inevitable that Werner would have been attacked and it would be in the media," Kamin said. "The media represents the voice of the current social, historical paradigm. Every era in history has its paradigm and those people who do not fit with the paradigm become the outlaws, the martyrs. When Galileo said the earth wasn't the center of the universe, he didn't fit with the paradigm of the Middle Ages," Kamin said.[4] Because Galileo challenged the established beliefs about the world during his time, he was subjected to the wrath of the church. He consequently spent the last eight years of his life under house arrest—confined to his home—in an attempt to keep him from spreading his blasphemy.

"The media becomes the medium for attack of anything that is extraordinary, anyone who is really great and anyone who really makes a difference," Kamin continued. "Werner is an unusual man, different. It's the ancient story—we have a tendency to crucify those people who don't fit with our understanding of the way things should operate. Werner created this great work that made a huge difference to a lot of people so, because it doesn't fit the current paradigm, it's characterized as pop psychology or a cult. He must be in it for the money or he must really be a Jim Jones," Kamin said.

"After John F. Kennedy's assassination, there were all these stories in the press that Kennedy was a womanizer, that he was immoral," said Kamin. "Of course, it would be of less interest to uncover why the facts of his assassination don't match the Warren Commission report. There was a news report that Martin Luther King Jr. plagiarized some paper in college, and contents of FBI files saying that he was a womanizer were leaked to the press. What the heck does that have to do with King's contribution to humanity? Martin Luther King was a giant in human history," Kamin said.

Kamin referred to Erhard's work in the area of ending hunger on the planet as an example of his outstanding contribution to humanity. "Werner's been a champion for what I would call the wretched of the earth for a very long time, and he didn't do that to make money," Kamin said. "Contrary to popular opinion, he didn't benefit financially from that. He didn't suck money from here or there. Werner was genuinely committed to the plight of people in India, Ethiopia, Cambodia, Bangladesh. He spearheaded an effort many years ago when there was a famine in Cambodia to make sure it was publicized. He raised some money to pay for ads around the country to let people know about that famine. He'd go to Ethiopia and come back and talk about what it was like being with those people. He insisted that everybody he knew donate money to relief organizations to immediately feed the people in Ethiopia. He started a project in India to purify the water that was killing babies there.

"The guy is committed. I've never seen Werner not be his word, not operate with a tremendous amount of dignity and integrity. He's unusual. I've never seen a man who's more committed to fulfilling what he sees makes a difference in anyone, contrary to the media image of Werner being motivated by greed, self interest and a desire to be viewed as a messiah.''

Kamin finds the charge that Erhard is a cult leader ridiculous. "I'm Jewish and I don't worship any other gods—I believe in just one god. I'm certainly no duped follower of an evil cult. And Werner is no cult leader.''[5]

Erhard also knows that he was a threat in some ways. "You know, we live in a culture in which the idea is—as the Australians say—to cut down the tall poppy. It scares the life out of certain people that somebody would be useful. Scares the life out of them,'' Erhard said. "That's hard for some people to believe because they're not frightened by useful people. But there are people who are crazy with fear of people who are useful. I mean they can't tolerate people who are useful and they attack them out of that fear. And I'm one of those guys who got attacked like that, by some of the people—even people in my family who never liked the fact that I was useful because it was threatening to them.''[6]

The people who worked the closest with Erhard over the years and came to know him very intimately say he was a truly remarkable person to work for and unlike anyone they had ever known. They appreciated his uniqueness and received enormous benefits from their experiences with him.

Jayne Sillari, a former school teacher, was one of only a handful of Erhard's aides from 1980 until he left the country in 1991. With the exception of his vacations which didn't happen very often and his sleeping time, Erhard always had an aide with him handling all the details of his busy schedule and staying in communication with his network. While the hours were long and the responsibility intense, Sillari said she loved working with Erhard.

"I have to say that Werner Erhard is the easiest person in the world to work with and work for. He means what he says, says what he means, there's no confusion, he's straight. All you have to do is be straight with him. The only time I ever got into trouble with him was when I wasn't straight, when I was hiding something that I didn't want to acknowledge." She recalled a time she screwed up some statistics she had prepared that Erhard was relying on to make a point.

"I was like, 'what am I going to do'. So we were driving somewhere, I was in the back seat and I knew I had to get this out of my mouth." She told him she had made a serious error by transposing some figures in the statistics he had just used in a big meeting and what she had done about it after the error had been called to her attention by one of the participants at the meeting.

"I told him I had called everybody at the meeting and I apologized for my mistake. This took a long time to get out of my mouth and he said 'Thank you'. I said 'I don't think you heard what I said' and I started to repeat myself. He turned around and he said 'You made a mistake, right? And you cleaned it up, didn't you? Well what more are you supposed to do?' "[7]

Bill Palmer became one of Erhard's aides in 1987. He had joined the staff two weeks after graduating from college with a degree in comparative literature in 1973 and worked in various capacities, including managing the center in Pittsburgh, coordinating the seminar leaders around the country, producing major events. Palmer said being Erhard's aid was the best job he had—and the most challenging. "It was insane for people to say Werner was excessive or eccentric," Palmer said. "He expected someone to do something with accuracy. Most people are sloppy and inaccurate and don't have integrity. Not Werner."[8]

Palmer was Erhard's aide when the media blitz hit. "It was a blow to him—a shock. Something off the wall was happening. But he never changed. He never got bitter or tried to take it out on people around him," Palmer said. "Werner amazed me. He was always the same—not like monotonous—but the public and private Werner were the same. He never allowed himself to be petty. When he made a mistake, he acknowledged it and moved on."

One of the most valuable lessons Palmer said he got from Erhard was that nothing was wrong. "Werner would see me about to make a mistake. Because he knew if I made that mistake, I'd learn a lot faster from it, he wouldn't stop me. He was the same way with his kids. He let them make mistakes. Werner always treated people like they were responsible for their own lives and either would have something work or not."[9]

For three of the four and a half years Palmer was Erhard's aide, Steve Self (no relation to the author) was also an aide. Self had done the training in 1978 while still a college student. Being an avid rock climber, Self decided he wanted to work with the 6-Day course after seeing a promotional film about it and subsequently participating in it. Self then decided he wanted to become a Forum Leader Candidate after six years on the 6-Day staff but thought maybe he should work directly with Erhard for a while first. He became an aide in 1985 and said that experience was the best training he ever received.

"It was very intense," Self said. "Werner was so completely committed to the truth and to things being spoken and represented as they really were. One had to choose to be in training and put one's point of view aside for the possibility of learning something. Werner was always straight with me."[10]

Kenneth Yamamoto, another of Erhard's personal aides during the late 1970s and off and on throughout the 1980s, found Erhard's unique style of management invaluable. "Werner just had a commitment to having things work. He would do whatever it takes to have everything work around him. Although people often misunderstood, Werner had a very deep commitment to people as human beings and to people having their lives work."[11]

Laurel Scheaf, currently a Forum Leader for Landmark Corporation, started working for Erhard when he was still at Parents. She helped him start the *est* training, becoming the first president of *est*. In 1967, Scheaf had left her home in Columbus, Ohio, after graduation from college looking for adventure. She said she found it when she met Erhard. "I loved working for Werner from the beginning. Werner had a technology of having people be effective," Scheaf said. "Although there were highs and lows and tough spots, there was never a time when Werner wasn't making a contribution. He was so committed to people being effective, he would get you whatever you needed any time, even sitting by your side for support if that's what was needed. Werner is the most intentional human being I've ever known."[12]

Rik Super, a former school teacher, joined Erhard's staff in 1982. In 1987 he was asked to manage Erhard's office and found the experience to be invaluable.

"The way Werner Erhard works rubs off on you.

He's extremely complete and thorough.'' Super had done a lot of reflecting on his relationship with Erhard and some serious soul-searching since all the allegations and accusations became public. He couldn't find any reason not to continue to completely trust the man who had made a profound difference in his life.

"If you're willing to work with someone who expects a lot of you, if you're willing to rise to the occasion that person presents, you can truly alter your life with that. Yes, you can get upset and walk away. But it may take a little bit more to be able to work with him, a little more strength, a little more courage to face up to your own weaknesses to change a little bit like a quarterback who may have a tough coach. . . . I have used the opportunity of having a coach like Werner who is demanding and insists on excellence and insists on the most from his people to get the value that is possible from that kind of interaction with somebody,'' said Super.[13]

Unfortunately, Erhard's opportunities to make such a profound difference with the people who are close to him as well as people halfway around the world from him have been seriously hampered. As his attorney, Walter Maksym, pointed out, "The public seems to love to see its heroes killed off. It's tragic that with the assassination of the character of this man, a lot of possibilities were lost, perhaps forever."[14]

[1] Interview with Mark Kamin, June 2, 1992.

[2] Interview with Mark Kamin, June 7, 1992.

[3] Kamin, June 7, 1992.

[4] Kamin, June 2, 1992.

[5] Interviews with Mark Kamin, June 2 and 7, 1992.

[6] Interview with Werner Erhard, September 15, 1991.

[7] Interview with Jayne Sillari, December 28, 1991

[8] Interview with Bill Palmer, June 6, 1992.

[9] Palmer, June 6, 1992.

[10] Interview with Steve Self, May 30, 1992.

[11] Interview with Kenneth Yamamoto, January 2, 1992.

[12] Interview with Laurel Scheaf, June 8, 1992.

[13] Interview with Rik Super, December 29, 1991.

[14] Interview with Walter Maksym, June 12, 1992.

CHAPTER XI
EPILOGUE

On March 3, 1992, Attorney Walter Maksym filed a multimillion dollar lawsuit in Chicago on behalf of Werner Erhard against CBS, *60 Minutes* producers David Gelber, Douglas Hamilton, and Donald Hewitt; the *National Enquirer; Hustler Magazine;* the Cult Awareness Network; Charlene Afremow, Randy Loftin, their attorney Andrew Wilson, Wendy and Vincent Drucker, Landon and Becky Carter; Robert Larzelere, Dawn Damas, Paul Gutfreund, and John Hubner alleging defamation of character, interference with prospective economic advantage, invasion of privacy, and conspiracy.

In an effort to provide an opportunity for the defendants to settle with Erhard, Maksym non-suited the case on May 29, 1992. "A non-suit allows the plaintiff to voluntarily dismiss a case and maintain the right to reinstate it within one year," explained Maksym. "If they choose not to work out a settlement, we will reinstate the suit."[1]

As this book is going to press, Erhard's daughter, Celeste Erhard, has begun legal action against John Hubner and the *San Jose Mercury News* for the way she was manipulated while in drug therapy with promises of great wealth so as to destroy her father's reputation.

While this story centered on a man named Werner Erhard, it also raised some serious questions about the role of the media. What we are sometimes led to believe in skillfully crafted reports is in stark contrast to the truth revealed by our own independent investigation, which the majority of people don't have the time or inclination to pursue. We depend on the press to provide the truth, the whole picture, to enable us to be functioning, free-thinking members of a democratic society.

Journalist/author Carl Bernstein recently pointed out in *The New Republic* that the press had abdicated its responsibility. "We need to start asking the same fundamental questions about the press that we do of the other powerful institutions in this society—about who is served, about standards, about self-interest and its eclipse of the public interest and the interest of truth. For the reality is that the media are probably the most powerful of all our institutions today; and they are squandering their power and ignoring their obligation."[2]

From the veranda of his friend's mountaintop home overlooking the Pacific Ocean in central Mexico, Erhard summarized the events that turned his life upside down. He expressed no animosity or anger toward his attackers, just surprise that it could have happened so swiftly and so viciously.

"I was personally stunned by this savage attack. How could one unscrupulous organization and a few individuals, hiding behind self-righteous justification, manipulate and coerce otherwise decent people and unleash the enormous power of the press to do their dirty work?'' Erhard said.

"On some basis, I can see how some individuals find themselves with justifications for acts they would normally find repulsive. I must trust that truth will ultimately speak for itself and that the ruthless exploitation of my family will stop. As for me, I will continue to focus my attention on doing whatever I can to heal my family, friends and associates, and get on with my life.''[3]

On reading all the articles from the Bay Area Press, and then reviewing the tape of *60 Minutes*, even after months of my own research I still found it hard to get it clear in my mind that there is not one bit of proof, not even one shred of hard evidence, that Erhard did any of the things alleged. There simply is no evidence to support the accusations. The only evidence ever offered were the accusations themselves. The people I have spoken to have come to the point where they really do not want to hear any more accusations, or accusations corroborated by nothing more than more accusations. They don't want any more stories implying wrongdoing, first they want to see one piece, any piece, of hard evidence.

This is a story of stark contrasts.

L. Ron Hubbard's Church of Scientology's paranoid old fantasies led them into a 17 year-long bizarre plot to destroy Werner Erhard. Werner Erhard, during the same time was working toward eliminating hunger and starvation in the world. In recognition of his work, he was honored with the "Mahatma Gandhi International Foundation's" Annual Humanitarian Award.

Charlene Afremow and Paul Gutfreund, hoping to extract millions for themselves from WE&A, using a handful of Erhard's former associates to generate frightful allegations against Erhard, attempted to force settlement of their suits, which suits they both substantially lost. In contrast, Werner Erhard, through the Werner Erhard Foundation gave in excess of four million dollars to concrete projects to relieve suffering and improve the quality of people's lives around the world.

Wendy and Vincent Drucker and their cohorts combed through thousands of Erhard's ex-employees and associates to find just 10 people, who would be willing to step forward to make defamatory allegations, later used in the press, against their former boss and friends. In response to just one article that featured the disaffected little group's complaints about working with Erhard's company, over 240 ex-employees and associates paid for an ad out of their own pockets, stating that what was said about working for Erhard was, "false, inaccurate, and misleading". They said, "The time we spent as employees was one of the richest experiences of our lives. We worked hard because we enjoyed our work and found it deeply satisfying."

Led by the *San Francisco Chronicle's* religious reporter, Don Lattin, a few members of the San Francisco press ballyhooed the defamatory accusations, hiding behind our legal system that in this case, never subjected the accusations to proof, and prevented a charge of libel from being brought against them for republication of the libelous statements made in the lawsuit. The newspapers effectively contravened the judge's intention when he sealed the scurrilous and irrelevant declarations. The San Francisco press gave no ink to the contradictory declarations, nor to the thousands of dedicated and satisfied employees and former employees who wanted to set the record straight and be heard about their experience of working in Erhard's organizations.

Ellen Erhard, who by her own admission felt small in comparison with her husband, poisoned the minds of Erhard's children against him and set in motion a turmoil which would turn a family, that once had parties just to celebrate life, into a disaster. Even with the brutal attack on Erhard, there is not one record of him ever saying anything derogatory about anyone in his family, or his associates or former associates.

Abdicating the duty that goes with enormous power, *60 Minutes*, arguably the most powerful news organization in the world, without one single piece of hard evidence for even one of the allegations they used as ammunition, turned its mighty guns on Erhard, and irresponsibly fired them at him point blank. Werner Erhard's only weapon was the truth.

Erhard had his own final words:

"We can't always dictate our personal circumstances, but we are always free to choose to what we will commit our lives. One can allow life to be used up by the circumstances or one can take the circumstances and choose to be free. Each of us makes the choice to either be fascinated by the soap opera, the folly of being human, or to celebrate life, the dignity of life, and the worth of each individual.

"Because each of us is, in the final analysis, nothing more than an ordinary human being, a man's unique story is ultimately trivial. Life can always be told as a story, but no matter how engrossing, what difference does a story make. Relieving another's suffering, contributing to another's joy is certainly one of the great privileges in life, but even this is not in itself uncommon.

"I've tried to live my life so that my life could be a place where the truth could go to work. Will the insights into the nature of being human, and beyond that, new possibilities of being for human beings result in any lasting value for life? Only time will tell. If there is anything uncommon, it is not the man but the ideas that have taken root in the life of the man.

"If I were allowed only one last word it would be to thank, with all my heart, the wonderful people who have given joy to my life with their friendship and support."[4]

[1] Interview with Walter Maksym, June 12, 1992.

[7] Carl Bernstein, "The Idiot Culture", The *New Republic*, June 8,1992.

[3] Interview with Werner Erhard, September 15, 1991.

[4] Interview with Werner Erhard, September 15, 1991.